TWENTIETH CENTURY
INTERPRETATIONS
OF

THE TURN OF THE SCREW
and Other Tales

TWENTIETH CENTURY INTERPRETATIONS OF THE TURN OF THE SCREW And Other Tales

A Collection of Critical Essays

Edited by
JANE P. TOMPKINS

Prentice-Hall, Inc. Englewood Cliffs, N. J.
A SPECTRUM BOOK

 C-13-933044-5; P-13-933036-4. *Library of Congress Catalog Card Number 73-126815.* Printed in the United States of America.

Current printing (last number):
10 9 8 7 6 5 4 3 2 1

Prentice-Hall International, Inc. (*London*)
Prentice-Hall of Australia, Pty. Ltd. (*Sydney*)
Prentice-Hall of Canada, Ltd. (*Toronto*)
Prentice-Hall of India Private Limited (*New Delhi*)
Prentice-Hall of Japan, Inc. (*Tokyo*)

Contents

TWENTIETH CENTURY
INTERPRETATIONS
OF

THE TURN OF THE SCREW
and Other Tales

Introduction

by Jane P. Tompkins

Henry James wrote to Robert Louis Stevenson in 1888 that he proposed "for a longish period, to do nothing but short lengths. I want to leave a multitude of pictures of my time, projecting my small circular frame upon as many different spots as possible and going in for number as well as quality. . . ."[1] James himself recognized that his strength as a writer lay in the depth and refinement of his portraits, not in their breadth and variety. By writing a series of vignettes, he may have felt that he could widen the range of his fiction, achieving a scope similar, perhaps, to that of the *Decameron* or the *Canterbury Tales*. "By doing short things I can do so many, touch so many subjects, break out in so many places, handle so many of the threads of life."[2] The hundred-odd tales James wrote over the course of his life cannot compare with Chaucer's or Boccaccio's for versatility and inclusiveness; they make their appeal on different grounds. Although his tales vary considerably in subject matter, mood, and technique, their claim to attention lies chiefly in the quality of the sensibility that informs them. The question is always what James will "do" with a given situation, what treasures of feeling, intelligence, and imagination he will disclose in the exploration of his chosen subject. As he said in his Preface to *The Awkward Age,* "the truth is that what a happy thought has to give depends immensely on the general turn of the mind capable of it. . . ."[3] James achieved scope and complexity through concentration of focus, and the virtues of his method—subtlety of analysis and an imaginative grasp of possibilities—are passed on to the attentive reader of his stories in the form of a broader awareness of life arrived at through sharper perceptions.

But if the experience of reading James's stories can intensify life to that extent, the experience of writing them was even more vivid. James's

[1] *The Letters of Henry James,* 2 vols., ed. Percy Lubbock (New York: Charles Scribner's Sons, 1920), I, 138.

[2] *The Notebooks of Henry James,* ed. F. O. Matthiessen and Kenneth B. Murdock (New York: Oxford University Press, 1947), p. 106.

[3] *The Novels and Tales of Henry James,* 25 vols. (New York: Charles Scribner's Sons, 1936), IX, viii.

Notebooks testify again and again to the fact that he lived his life largely through his fiction. "To live *in* the world of creation . . . —this is the only thing." [4] The fullness and intensity of that creative life, and the high excitement of it, account in part for the apparent meagerness of his biography.

James felt himself, both in relation to his brilliant family and to the world at large, a "small vague outsider." This feeling is described in one of the autobiographical works that he wrote near the end of his career, in a passage analyzing his relation to other children.

> They were so *other*—that was what I felt; and to *be* other, other almost anyhow, seemed as good as the probable taste of the bright compound wistfully watched in the confectioner's window. . . . I never dreamed of competing—a business having in it at the best, for my temper, if not for my total failure of temper, a displeasing ferocity. . . . It wasn't that I wished to change with everyone, with anyone at a venture, but that I saw "gifts" everywhere but as mine and that I scarce know whether to call the effect of this miserable or monstrous. It was the effect at least of self-abandonment—I mean to visions.[5]

The young James seems naturally to have fallen into the role of an observer, keenly appreciative of the riches in the life around him, but divided from them by an invisible barrier. Brought up in Albany and New York City until the age of twelve, he spent his adolescent years in Europe, absorbing its culture from books, art galleries, and theaters as his family moved from capital to resort. This nomadic cosmopolitan life must have lent itself readily to his spectator's habit of hoarding impressions and furnished him richly with the raw stuff of his "visions."

By the spring of 1861, when Lincoln issued his first call for volunteers, Henry was eighteen and the Jameses had returned to America, but a painful back injury he had sustained while helping to put out a fire kept him from enlisting. The accident "had sufficed . . . to establish a relation—a relation to everything occurring round me not only for the next four years but for long afterward. . . ." [6] At a time when James felt that "the likely young should be up and doing," [7] his inability to join those who were leaving for the front confirmed his sense of helpless otherness. Perhaps for the lack of anything better to do, James followed the lead of his older brother, William, and studied art in Newport; then, a year and a half later, he migrated to Cambridge, where William had preceded him, and began to attend classes

[4] *Notebooks,* p. 112.
[5] *A Small Boy and Others* (New York: Charles Scribner's Sons, 1913), pp. 175–76.
[6] *Notes of a Son and Brother* (New York: Charles Scribner's Sons, 1914), p. 297.
[7] Ibid.

at Harvard Law School. But neither of these ventures seems to have engaged him seriously; instead of studying law he devoted himself to writing, and in 1864 the *Continental Monthly* published his first story, "A Tragedy of Error."

The unsigned story was followed by a series of book and theater reviews, articles on art and travel, and more stories. James's talent had begun to jell, but he felt the need of a more congenial atmosphere. Two more extended visits to Europe decided him in favor of the Old World, and in 1876 he established himself, more or less permanently, in London. In the same year he published *Roderick Hudson,* a novel about the experience of an American artist in Europe, and from this point forward the volume of his journalism declined and his output of fiction steadily rose. His observation post as a cultivated expatriate supplied him with a rich array of subjects, most of which revolved thematically around the encounter between American and European values: between innocence and experience, morality and tradition, freedom and restraint, life and art. The impressions he gathered as a dinner guest and weekend visitor in homes that received the cream of European society were transformed into novels and stories by his imaginative gift for seeing "into" the social situation. Among the features of James's own life reflected in his fiction is its lack of surface incident. Whatever there is of drama and heroism in his novels almost invariably takes the form of visions, renunciations, and disciplines, intensely private and concealed from the outward eye. The vicissitudes of James's personal life were likewise shielded from public view. He wrote, dined out, visited friends, and continued to travel, recrossing the Atlantic periodically. But, with the exception of his unsuccessful attempt to write for the stage, and the deaths of friends and members of his family, his life was unmarked by climactic events until the outbreak of the war, and by then it was nearly over.

World War I gave James the opportunity, which he had always deliberately shunned (but perhaps secretly longed for), to abandon the isolation of the observer and make common cause with ordinary men. At this juncture, an element of heroism does appear in the visible picture. In an effort to lend his moral weight to the Allies, James became a British citizen in 1915. We find him, moreover, past seventy, with a bad heart, constantly visiting the bedsides of the wounded who crowded the London hospitals and framing fund-raising appeals designed to move a general public he had long since despaired of reaching in his fiction. James's change of citizenship in wartime was a symbolic gesture of commitment to a public cause that seems uncharacteristic of him; all his life he had refrained from public gestures of any kind. But as Virginia Woolf saw in her review of *Within the Rim* (a collection of James's essays about the war), the cause which he embraced in 1914 was in essence the same one he had always hoped to advance as a writer of fiction.

> It was Belgium, it was France, it was above all England and the English tradition, it was everything he had ever cared for of civilization, beauty and art threatened with destruction and arrayed before his imagination in one figure of tragic appeal.[8]

In recognizing the continuity of purpose that unites James's support of the Allies with his literary pursuits, Virginia Woolf shows an understanding of his work that was not shared by most of his contemporaries. Although he won the steady admiration of a few critics and eventually acquired a small coterie of devoted followers, during his lifetime his fiction never provoked the curiosity and reverence it commands today. Moreover, the qualities that his readers found objectionable then are frequently the same ones that make his work attractive now. He was considered too analytical and pessimistic; his characters did not elicit unqualified sympathy; the good were not rewarded and the bad escaped punishment; and his plots ended inconclusively.[9]

The moral complexity and psychological subtlety that appeal to modern readers of James are manifest in his short fiction as well as in his novels. Since he worked at short things over the whole span of his career, the tales touch upon all of his major themes. They also provide a measure of his technical skill, since he achieved particular success in the genre known as the *novella,* or long short story. James referred to the form as the "blest *nouvelle,*" because while it demanded economy, it gave him room to develop the possibilities of his subject. Accordingly, he distinguished the *nouvelle* from the "anecdote" or short story, which, he felt, narrowly restricted the range of imaginative exploration. Although he constantly attempted short pieces because they were easier to place in the magazines than longer works, often, as the possibilities of his "germ" unfolded themselves, his stories stretched far beyond the 5,000 word limit imposed by contemporary editors. Five of the six stories discussed in this volume approach or attain the length of *nouvelles;* only one, "The Real Thing," can be called an "anecdote." Although the stories have been selected chiefly on the basis of their popularity, they touch on the major themes of the Jamesian canon, and since these themes are interlocked, the stories have a common frame of reference. Read as a sequence, they illumi-

[8] Virginia Woolf, "Within the Rim," in *The Death of the Moth and Other Essays* (New York: Harcourt, Brace and Company, 1942), pp. 129–30.

[9] Roger Gard, *Henry James: The Critical Heritage* (London: Routledge and Kegan Paul, Ltd., 1968), pp. 5–6.

nate one another, and questions of interpretation such as those that are raised in the following pages can often be resolved by a process of mutual comparison. At the price, then, of ignoring differences in tone, method, and emphasis, it will be useful to trace briefly the features that give the stories their family resemblance.

All of the stories lead up to or center around one revelatory moment in which a character sees or has forced upon him a truth that changes his life. For the purposes of this discussion it will be best to start with the later tales and work backward since they focus on this motif more exclusively than the others. "The Beast in the Jungle" (1903) is almost unique in its explicit statement of the meaning of the crucial vision, and so furnishes a key for deciphering more obscure revelations in the other tales.

After a lifetime of speculating, in the company of a sympathetic woman, on the form his peculiar destiny will take, John Marcher discovers that his destiny had consisted of nothing more than his attenuated expectation of it. When the woman who had waited with him has been dead for some time, he suddenly realizes:

> The escape would have been to love her; then, *then* he would have lived. *She* had lived—who could say now with what passion?—since she had loved him for himself; whereas he had never thought of her (ah, how it hugely glared at him!) but in the chill of his egotism and the light of her use.[10]

The substance of Marcher's vision is that in failing to love May he has failed to live. The man incapable of loving is spiritually dead in James's eyes, and he reinforces the equation by stating it positively as well as negatively: May had lived since she had loved Marcher for himself. This central truth remains a constant in James's fiction, while the ways in which his characters evade it vary. In "The Beast in the Jungle," Marcher's romanticized picture of his life has kept him from seeing its actual meagerness. Living vicariously through his fantasies of peril and disaster, he never acts in the present, and when he awakens from his dream it is too late. This tendency toward romantic idealization of the self limits the understanding and consequently the experience of other Jamesian protagonists as well.

The chief of Marcher's fantasies, the metaphor of the hunt which gives "The Beast in the Jungle" its title, is acted out by the hero of "The Jolly Corner" (1908). The passionate self which Marcher refused to acknowledge haunted him mentally in the form of a beast; for Spencer Brydon it takes the form of a man whom Brydon stalks through the narrow corridors and back rooms of his ancestral house.

[10] *The Complete Tales of Henry James,* 12 vols., ed. Leon Edel (New York: J. B. Lippincott Company, 1964), XI, 401–2.

The sensations each man experiences in the confrontation with his hidden self are strikingly similar. Marcher's encounter with the beast overwhelms his shadowy identity; in all but the physical sense he dies as a result of his vision. But for Spencer Brydon, although the vision of his alter ego is devastating, it brings about an emotional rebirth. The two sides of his personality, which had become dissociated when he left home thirty years before, have fused, and he is now capable of loving the woman who has waited for him: his May Bartram is still alive, the door still open. The identification between loving and living made in "The Beast in the Jungle" gathers new meaning here. James's language suggests that Brydon has not simply come back to life physically and emotionally, but has been born again in the biblical sense. Alice Staverton, all gentle and forgiving, shows an angelic acceptance of the monstrous potentialities in his nature; it is as though, awakening in the soft pillow of her lap, he has been received into the divine embrace. The love that Brydon's ordeal has made possible for him, in other words, is a form of salvation itself.

The relation between love and death and sudden vision remains below the surface of "The Figure in the Carpet" (1896), but it governs the convolutions of the plot. George Corvick's discovery of the secret of Vereker's novels is due, James hints, to his love for Gwendolyn Erme. Moreover, it is suggested that Corvick withholds the secret from her until the intimacies of their wedding night. When the narrator tells Gwendolyn later that he thinks the "figure" is a hoax, she declares: "It's my *life!*" The suggestion that "life" involves the experience of loving may be only obscurely indicated here, but the evidence of "The Beast in the Jungle" and "The Jolly Corner" makes that inference plausible.[11] The successive deaths of those who know the meaning of the figure—Hugh Vereker, his wife, George Corvick, and Gwendolyn Erme—suggest, moreover, that the price of this life-giving secret is, paradoxically, life itself. James's view of the consequences of vision changed over a period of years. For the characters in "The Figure in the Carpet," as for John Marcher, the experience is ultimately fatal, and although James hints at its redemptive value, this possibility is not fully developed until later, in *The Golden Bowl,* and, as we have seen, "The Jolly Corner."

The discovery made by the narrator of "The Real Thing" (1892) does not concern love so much as the human capacity for courage and humility. The narrator in this story saw Major and Mrs. Monarch at

[11] Several critics are in agreement on this point. See Seymour Lainoff, "Henry James' 'The Figure in the Carpet': What is Critical Responsiveness?" in the present collection; Leo B. Levy, "A Reading of 'The Figure in the Carpet,'" *American Literature,* XXXIII, no. 4 (1962), 459; and Parker Tyler, "The Figure in the Carpet," in *Every Artist His Own Scandal* (New York: Horizon Press, 1964), p. 231.

first as social "types" of the sort represented in the novels he illustrated, and so remained unaware of their real value. In the instant that he perceives them as human beings and sees the drama of their personal lives, their true worth shines out at him, and simultaneously he becomes aware of the superficiality of his own work. Like the narrator-critic of "The Figure in the Carpet," the illustrator's conception of art has been limited by his ignorance of life. The cost of vision in "The Real Thing" is not so high as in the other tales because the revelation is less intimate and profound, but the principle that controls the action is the same. The artist has had a glimpse of life at a new level of intensity and has had to pay for the privilege with a permanently damaged style. Yet, as in all of the foregoing stories, James makes us feel that the knowledge gained is infinitely precious, and that even if the price is life itself, *not* to have seen would have been a worse fate still.

"The Pupil" (1891) is perhaps an exception to this norm. Morgan Moreen had often dreamed that one day, like the hero of an adventure story, he would run away from his shabby family and live happily ever after with his tutor, whom he idolized. The realization that instead of rejecting his parents he has been rejected by them, and worse yet, by Pemberton, his tutor, smashes his illusions and kills him. The shock that destroys his weak heart results in part from his storybook conception of himself: as James remarks, "the turn taken was away from a *good* boy's book." In this respect, Morgan resembles John Marcher, whose life of vain imaginations left him too weak to withstand the shock of truth. Morgan, like Marcher, is intellectually sophisticated but emotionally immature; however, because he is still a boy, he cannot be held responsible for his unwillingness to face his isolation. The moral failure lies with Pemberton and the Moreens. Their insensitivity to Morgan's feelings, and their lack of love for him, are responsible for his death. In Marcher's case, it is the failure of love in himself that appalls; what destroys Morgan is the failure of love in others.

The Turn of the Screw (1898) seems to offer an ironic inversion of the pattern traced so far. The elements of love, death, and sudden vision remain constant, but their values appear to have been hideously transformed. In the other stories a central character has an instantaneous glimpse of a truth whose meaning is often shrouded and ambiguous; the governess at Bly receives not one but half a dozen such astounding visitations, of whose significance she is intuitively sure. In the other tales the vision discloses something about the nature and importance of human love; for the governess, the knowledge acquired concerns demonic possession, and, it is hinted, sexual perversion. Nor does her repeated exposure to such visions have any lasting effects as far as she herself is concerned; rather, it causes the death of one of her charges and the temporary derangement of the other. These distortions of the characteristic visionary experience make the governess's tale seem a sinister parody of James's recurrent theme. Always a threat to mortal affairs, the encounter with the numinous realm in this instance looses a destructive force that shocks to numbness, while it totally lacks the sanative, if caustic, effect that revelation has in most of the other tales. The reason for this frightening mutation of the theme is implied in Miles's gasping exclamation at the end: "Peter Quint—you devil!" If the words "you devil" refer to the governess, this suggests that it is she herself who is the servant of evil, and not the ghosts who visit her. And if the governess, because of her psychic needs, has herself originated the maleficent influences she is striving to thwart, then her encounters with Miss Jessel and Peter Quint are a diseased caricature of genuine vision, and the real parallel between *The Turn of the Screw* and the other stories lies in the flash of insight that comes to Miles at the climax. The resemblance to the concluding episode of "The Pupil" is worth noting. Again, the elements of love and death are intertwined. The startling perception that killed Morgan Moreen involved an awareness that those on whom he had counted most for love and protection have proved callous or tepid in their feelings. Miles suffers from the opposite realization. It is the governess's obsessive desire to possess him totally that frightens him to death. But even if one does not agree that the governess is responsible for the catastrophe, and blames the ghost, as she does, the cause of Miles's death remains the same: both Peter Quint and the governess direct at the defenseless child the perverted love of a frustrated adulthood.

The sudden insight which transposes the lives of James's characters into a new key or blots them out entirely always breaks in from the outside. This is most obvious in "The Pupil" and *The Turn of the Screw,* but even in those stories where the protagonist consciously seeks illumination, the truth waits to flash upon him until the seeker has momentarily turned his back. Ironically, the momentous vision, without which a man is deprived of life in its deepest sense, cannot be had by an effort of will. Like divine grace, it is bestowed at the discretion of a higher power. George Corvick discovers the meaning of the figure in the carpet when he has given up the search and gone to India. Marcher learns the nature of his fate as the result of a chance occurrence: "It had not come to him, the knowledge, on the wings of experience; it had brushed him, jostled him, upset him, with the disrespect of chance, the insolence of an accident." [12] And Spencer Brydon, the most self-conscious and resolute of all the seekers, meets his alter

[12] James, *Complete Tales,* XI, 401.

ego only after his nerve has failed him and he has decided to abandon the search for good.

The irony that marks each of these discoveries also stamps itself on the crucial episodes of "The Pupil," "The Real Thing," and *The Turn of the Screw*. Although Morgan Moreen had for some time been aware of the seedy morality of his parents, it is his trusted ally, Pemberton, who lets him down in the end. Major and Mrs. Monarch, rejected by the narrator as models for his bread-and-butter sketches, inadvertently show him, through the nobility of their conduct, what the subject of his art ought to be. And the governess at Bly, who believes she is heroically protecting Miles and Flora from the evil that threatens them, becomes herself an unwitting angel of death.

However, as we have seen, James's irony even at its harshest usually avoids cynicism because the ironic event is the occasion for a revelation of truth. Although the revelation is often terrifying, in most cases it comes as a welcome relief. The crystallization of doubt into fact banishes hovering alternatives, lifts the burden of tension, and conveys a sense of achievement, so that knowing the truth seems infinitely preferable to remaining in a state of uncertainty or ignorance. This sense of final clarity and consummation is partly a product of James's narrative technique, but it stems also from the kinds of values he establishes in his stories.

All of the stories present life on two levels of awareness: life as it is ordinarily lived, and life experienced in its greatest depth and intensity. The visionary moment, which marks an entrance into the realm of intenser being, comes only to a few and is paid for in suffering or death. The pattern might also be described in various, yet similar, ways: Unless a man be born again, not of the flesh but of the spirit, he cannot enter into the kingdom of Heaven; many are called but few are chosen; strait is the gate and narrow is the way; he who would save his life must lose it. It hardly follows from these New Testament parallels that a Christian philosophy of salvation lies at the heart of James's fiction. The analogy does, however, make one sensitive to the religious overtones of the vision James's characters share. They are in some sense initiates of a mystery, the nature of which is usually implied rather than stated, and in which the reader may participate only insofar as he is able to infer its content for himself.

Hugh Vereker cannot communicate the meaning of the figure apart from the living dramatization his novels have given it. May Bartram, who is herself the answer Marcher seeks, must offer herself to him in silence. And Alice Staverton, who has met Brydon's alter ego, can never share its significance with him until he has encountered it himself. The truth must come in its own form, of its own accord, and must be apprehended personally. It cannot be had secondhand because, as with mystical vision, there are no terms for communicating it.

The nature of James's theme forces one to adopt a mystical vocabulary in describing it, but for James himself the mystery is something essentially human. Whatever there is of the preternatural in his fictional world manifests itself in human form, the visionary experience being tied, in each case, to a relationship among persons. This is because James's own most profound intuitions seem to have come to him in dramatic form. His novels and tales tend to pivot around a series of theatrically conceived encounters, and he entrusts his central insights to images unusually dynamic and concrete: the leap of a beast, the breaking of a golden bowl. The critic, therefore, in dealing with these works, is likely to find himself at a loss for words, since the meanings James has trapped into the action—of the image and the scene—have no other channel of escape.

James's "The Pupil": The Art of Seeing Through

by Terence J. Martin

In his preface to "The Pupil" (1891) Henry James admits to an "incorrigible taste for gradations and superpositions of effect," to a "love, when it is a question of picture, of anything that makes for proportion and dimension, that contributes to a view of *all* the dimensions." He is, he continues, "addicted to seeing 'through'—one thing through another, accordingly, and still other things through *that*."[1] These remarks have a relevance to much of James's work: one sees, for example, the feminism of Boston through Basil Ransom, the innocence of Daisy Miller through Winterbourne, the experience of Paris through Lambert Strether, the egocentric adult warfare of the Faranges through Maisie. And in each case the manner of viewing contributes to one's knowledge of the viewer. In "The Pupil" the idea of "seeing through" is especially relevant and its application rewarding, for the structure of the story consists of a group of interdependent revelations which at once define the characters and dramatize the situation. "The Pupil" is built on "seeing through" in the double sense of the term: it is, as James tells us, through Pemberton that we see Morgan Moreen, through Morgan that we see the rest of the family; and it is through Pemberton and Morgan that we come to *see through* the Moreens and ultimately through Pemberton himself. James gives us "a view of *all* the dimensions" with a vengeance. The story reaches its climax and its conclusion at the point of absolute revelation, when there is no more seeing through to be done.

---

[1] *Henry James: Selected Fiction,* ed. Leon Edel (Everyman's Library, New York: E. P. Dutton & Co., 1953), pp. 479–80. All future references to "The Pupil" are to page numbers in this edition, cited parenthetically in the text.

To James the Moreens exemplify a part of the "copious 'cosmopolite' legend" which he terms "a boundless and tangled, but highly explorable, garden" (478). They are "of the family . . . of the great unstudied precursors—poor and shabby members, no doubt; dim and superseded types." The Moreens, that is, are a very early portrait of the American cosmopolite in Europe, "mediaeval," says James, "in the sense of being, at most, of the mid-century." Because they have been superseded by more standardized portraits, they and their experiences represent for the artist "a gold-mine overgrown and smothered, dislocated, and no longer workable" (479).

The Moreens, then, occupy the position of explorers—they belong to years "of prodigious and unrecorded adventure" (479). James will reach back into a kind of pre-history and tell us of their explorations. In the story itself Pemberton, whose consciousness operates to determine the point of view, sees them as an ignoble type of explorer: they are "adventurers," he believes, "not merely because they didn't pay their debts, because they lived on society, but because their whole view of life, dim and confused and instinctive, like that of other colour-blind animals, was speculative and rapacious and mean" (438–39). They are foragers, the first backwash of America to Europe. But since they cannot afford to be known for what they are, they must constantly be on the alert so as not to be seen through.

James's method of characterizing the Moreens begins typically enough with their name; identity and characterization are one in the name. Moreen is a fabric of coarse, stout wool or wool and cotton; usually it is watered or embossed. In short, it presents one kind of surface to the eye when underneath it is intrinsically coarse. The description fits the Moreen family precisely. They maintain a constant vigilance against "public exposure" which is an endless struggle not to be known for what they are, for they are, unequivocally, moreen. In the light of this we may see why James stresses repeatedly in the story that they are always "looking out": "looking out" is both a safeguard against being known by others and a way not to face the truth that is inside. The first meaning is explicit throughout the story; the second is implicit and equally obvious. "That was what he [Mr. Moreen] went off for," writes James, "to London and other places—to look out; and this vigilance was the theory of life, as well as the real occupation, of the whole family. They all looked out, for they were very frank on the subject of its being necessary" (425). James also makes it clear—by reiteration—that the dominant posture of Mr. Moreen and his elder son Ulick is that of "men of the world." And the "occupation" and the posture are brought together humorously and mournfully when, on a "sad November day" in Venice, with the wind roaring and the family fortunes at low ebb, Pemberton sees Mr.

Moreen and Ulick "in the Piazza, looking out for something, strolling drearily, in mackintoshes, under the arcade; but still, in spite of mackintoshes, unmistakable men of the world" (458). The "occupation" and the posture become one, embodied in the fake existence of the Moreens, an existence maintained only by not being revealed. . . .

The details of the daily life of the Moreens support James's initial name-characterization. They have a family language, called Ultramoreen by Morgan, which Pemberton defines as a kind of Volapük, a personal world language of ultra-fakery. As their financial position grows steadily worse, Mrs. Moreen refuses to buy new clothes for Morgan. "She did nothing that didn't show, neglected him because he escaped notice, and then, as he illustrated this clever policy, discouraged at home his public appearances. Her position was logical enough —those members of her family who did show had to be showy" (435). Mr. Moreen, with his white moustache and confiding manner, wears in his buttonhole "the ribbon of a foreign order—bestowed, as Pemberton eventually learned, for services." But "for what services he never clearly ascertained" (425). They live on "macaroni and coffee" (427), and it is probable that James is here playing on the word "maccaroni" to suggest additionally their dandified outward appearance. It becomes clear that they glitter on the surface, that their ways—as seen by Pemberton—are seductive and winning, but that the glitter is a part of their essential hypocrisy.

As the Moreens slide inexorably into a kind of indigence which ultimately makes it impossible for them to cover up, to hide their identity, they begin to strain and press too hard in their efforts to maintain a smoothness of surface. James employs the image of hands at several points in the story to suggest the moral tone of his portrait (and these images heighten the meaning of the Moreens' "eagerness to wash their hands" of Morgan [429], and Pemberton's later fear that he will have Morgan "on his hands" [468]). When Pemberton first meets Mrs. Moreen, he sees a "large affable lady" drawing "a pair of soiled *gants de Suède* through a fat jewelled hand . . ." (420). Later in the interview she puts out "a practised but ineffectual hand" to caress Morgan (422). Although the family continue to meet the world good-naturedly, they become "as good-natured as Jews at the doors of clothing shops" (456). The decline from *jew*elled hand to clothing-shop Jews measures their increasing obviousness. For the standard image of the Jew at the door of a clothing shop is that of a man rubbing his hands in hope of profit (he is literally "looking out" for trade), willing to agree, ready to turn on the blue light if the buyer wants a blue suit. James visits all the obviousness of this stock figure on the Moreens. In the final scene of the story Mrs. Moreen is "slowly rubbing her plump white hands" (474) while she urges Pemberton to take

Morgan off their hands. And when Morgan collapses, clutching at his heart, Mrs. Moreen cries out, "Help, help! he's going, he's gone" (475), a cry redolent of that of the auctioneer, whose professional pretext is of course that he is reluctant to part with the item, but who is understood as a man who puts a price on things, who will sell. At this point in the story there is no more surface; the Moreens have assumed their full identity after struggling with mounting desperation to conceal it.

"All I have given in 'The Pupil,'" says James, "is little Morgan's troubled vision of them [the Moreens] as reflected in the vision, also troubled enough, of his devoted friend" (479). But in giving us this much James has of course given us more; in seeing what the pupil sees we come to see the pupil and Pemberton as well.

Morgan, as we know, is entirely out of place in so mendacious a family; James's portrayal of him never allows us to forget this fact. Literally, the name Morgan signifies a dweller on the sea, and such a literal meaning applies to Morgan Moreen. Condemned to being with his family but not of them, to being in their world but not of it, Morgan is a nomad, a person eternally homeless. But the name might also suggest something further about his relationship to his family, for with the addition of a suffix the world becomes morganatic. In this form the name suggests a richly ironic relationship which is supported by the dramatic context of the story. In a morganatic relationship (usually marriage) the inferior partner does not acquire the rank, the title, the worldly position of the superior; in "The Pupil" Morgan does not acquire the heritage of moreen that belongs by right of identity to the rest of the family: he does not inherit the occupation of looking out or the man-of-the-world pose; he is not, that is, growing up to be a hypocrite and a fraud. But the word morganatic suggests a fuller meaning if one inverts the relationship: clearly Morgan is the superior member of the family; he alone possesses honesty and wisdom, he alone has *in*sight, he alone is the pupil. And just as these traits are age-old ideals, so by possessing them is Morgan much older than his family. He feels this himself and makes others feel it. During his initial interview with Pemberton, Morgan says that Ulick, eight years his senior, tries to imitate him. From the beginning Pemberton notices that "from one moment to the other his [Morgan's] small satiric face seemed to change its time of life" (422). Throughout the story Morgan feels a responsibility for what he cannot explain about his family: "What the boy couldn't get over was the fact that this particular blight seemed, in a tradition of self-respect, so undeserved and arbitrary. No doubt people had a right to take the line they liked, but why should *his* people have liked the line of pushing and toadying and lying and cheating? What had their forefathers—all decent folk, so far as he knew—done to them, or what had *he* done to them" (456)? They are *his* people; he wonders what *he* has done to them. Morgan has an ancestral view of the family. He is a child who embodies tradition, an old child, wise but perplexed at what *his* family has become.

James makes a point of saying that Morgan "rarely condescended" to speak Ultramoreen. In the original form of the story in *Longman's* James added "though he attempted colloquial Latin as if he had been a little prelate"; in revised form the phrase reads "though he dealt in colloquial Latin . . ." (428). The change from "attempted" to "dealt in" places a greater emphasis on Morgan's knowledge of Latin and consequently a greater emphasis on his difference from his family. Morgan is the *praelatus* or ruler of his family who has, in Latin, an old but authentic kind of Volapük. From the fact that Latin is a dead language, however, we can infer the ultimate hopelessness of Morgan's position.

James portrays this wise and learned child as a remarkable blend of intelligence and innocence (during their first interview Pemberton notes Morgan's "intelligent innocent eyes" [422]). He possesses "a whole range of refinement and perception—little musical vibrations as taking as picked-up airs—begotten by wandering about Europe at the tail of his migratory tribe." He has "a small strain of stoicism, doubtless the fruit of having had to begin early to bear pain." But although he has "noticed more things than you might suppose," he nevertheless has "his proper playroom of superstitions, where he smashed a dozen toys a day" (430).

Morgan has drawn from experience a mature knowledge of his family and himself: "It was as if he had been a little gentleman and had paid the penalty by discovering that he was the only such person in his family. This comparison didn't make him vain, but it could make him melancholy and a trifle austere" (450). However, Morgan is innocent as well as intelligent, and his knowledge, like the knowledge of all of us, has limits. Thus, in answer to Pemberton's " 'You *do* know everything,' " he cries out,

> "No I don't after all. I don't know what they live on, or how they live, or *why* they live! What have they got and how did they get it? Are they rich, are they poor, or have they a *modeste aisance?* Why are they always chiveying me about—living one year like ambassadors and the next like paupers? Who are they, anyway, and what are they? I've thought of all that—I've thought of a lot of things. They're so beastly worldly. That's what I hate most—oh I've *seen* it! All they care about is to make an appearance and to pass for something or other. What the dickens do they want to pass for? What *do* they, Mr. Pemberton?" (452)

These are questions that Pemberton cannot answer, as no one could. "Why aren't my people better people?" is substantially what Morgan is asking, and like many other things about Morgan, this question too is age-old. But these are not the questions of a child; they are not, for example, the questions of a Maisie Farange. Morgan's questions presume a vast intelligence; they are filled with intelligence, and when we see their meaning we see that it is Morgan's meaning. If Maisie were to ask analogous questions we would see more than she would. Maisie too sees through, but not always consciously; her vision is one of unconscious irony. Morgan knows exactly what he sees and where his knowledge leaves off. To answer the questions which he poses, he would have to be a man like George Bernard Shaw's Caesar; and although Morgan is old, he is not that old. " 'Who are they, anyway, and what are they?' " A frightening intelligence based on innocence underlies these words (they are questions we might ask of many people if we dared)—Morgan questions the identity of his parents and in doing so defines himself more completely as a dweller on the sea. Only when his parents' full identity is revealed to the world can he judge the gulf that separates him from his family. And the implications of this insight contribute heavily to his death.

Morgan is plagued by a weak heart that will keep him from growing up, that suggests, additionally, the tremendous lack of love that has always been his lot. But the fact is that Morgan could never "grow up" in the ordinary sense of the term. He is old already. He dies not the death of youth, of unfulfilled hope and promise and future, but the death of age, broken by disappointment, dismayed at the failure of love.

To Morgan, Pemberton seems to offer the fullest chance at life and love that he has ever had. For Pemberton loves Morgan, and when he comes to see the way in which the family uses his pupil, and Morgan's own knowledge of this, he stays on without pay as long as he can out of love or what seems to be love. But he is not entirely unaffected by the experience of living with such a family: he has a "sneaking kindness" (457) for the Moreens; their undeniable surface charm engages him. As a consequence, he finds himself beginning to deal with them on their own level. His speech takes on their "borrowed grace of idiom" (460); his talks with Mrs. Moreen are replete with a subtle diplomacy which he at once deplores and employs. And "part of the abasement of living with such people" is "that one had to make vulgar retorts, quite out of one's own tradition of good manners" (461).

Morgan urges Pemberton to leave, to save himself. He tells Pemberton of Zénobie, a nurse the family "hired" when he was younger, who also loved him, but who finally had to leave to get some money. Pemberton suggests (more as a wish than as a plan of action) that they " 'ought to go off and live somewhere together' " (449). When Pemberton, at Morgan's insistence, finally accepts an offer to "coach an opulent youth" in England on his own terms, he says, " 'I'll make a tremendous charge; I'll earn a lot of money in a short time, and we'll live on it' " (462). (Yet, in an earlier moment of imaginative reflection Pemberton has been unable to conceive of supporting Morgan: "He, Pemberton, might live on Morgan; but how could Morgan live on *him?*" [459]). Morgan's position in his family, his insight into that position, and his selfless devotion to Pemberton call forth a response from the tutor: "Pemberton held him fast, hands on his shoulders—he had never loved him so" (462).

In the context of such love and attention Morgan's health blooms. " 'Haven't you noticed,' " he asks Pemberton, " 'that there hasn't been a doctor near me since you came?' " " '*I'm* your doctor,' " Pemberton replies, "taking his arm and drawing him tenderly on again." Ominously, however, this statement is preceded by Pemberton's saying to Morgan in jest: " 'My dear fellow, you're too clever to live' "; " 'You *are* too clever to live' "; and " 'Look out or I'll poison you' " (453–54).

Pemberton returns to the Moreens from England in response to an urgent and fraudulent appeal from Mrs. Moreen regarding Morgan's health. At this point there is a curious change in his relationship to Morgan; for the remainder of the story he is a passive figure, no longer talking of the future, simply waiting to see what will happen. When Mrs. Moreen excuses her scheme for getting him back on the grounds that Pemberton has already taken Morgan away from his family, he is indignant. When Morgan pleads " 'Take me away—take me away,' " Pemberton replies with " 'where' " and " 'how' " (467). He feels that he is "in for it," that Morgan will be "on his hands again indefinitely" (468). He begins to feel "his collar gall him." He realizes that Morgan, out of gratitude for his return, will give him his life, but "what could he do with Morgan's dreadful little life?" (471). There is, in short, a radical change in Pemberton's attitude toward Morgan. What appeared to be love (which is what Morgan is counting on) is gone.

I believe that this change in attitude further defines Pemberton's initial attitude toward Morgan; in the light of his later passivity we may see the terms of his earlier apparently more aggressive affection. After Pemberton returns to the family, Morgan repeatedly refers to the future (their future); he reiterates what he takes to be their mutual desire, that Pemberton take him away. He thus forces Pemberton to think practically of these matters. But this is something that, despite his words, Pemberton has never really been able to do, and Morgan's insistence serves only to force him into passivity. Pemberton loves Morgan as Morgan exists in one particular situation; he loves the victimized Morgan. For the object of his love to insist on the chance of not being a victim, and to look to Pemberton to save (de-victimize) him, is to challenge the whole basis of the love relationship.

To say that Pemberton's role is that of a doctor would not be entirely correct; the evidence of the story suggests a more ambiguous role. Pemberton is a successor to the nurse Zénobie; his functions throughout are more those of a nurse than of a doctor. He would be a doctor, he claims to be, but he is not: he emerges, finally, as a passive and dependent figure—one whose function it is to nurse rather than to doctor. Indeed, his lack of independence breeds his "sneaking kindness" toward the Moreens, for "they were so out of the workaday world and kept him so out of it" (457). He has, we recall, been unable to conceive of supporting Morgan, though he can conceive of Morgan supporting him. Mrs. Moreen quite rightly senses his role of nursemaid when she says that Pemberton's place is with Morgan and the family, that he belongs in his place. Her insight increases his dissatisfaction, for he now sees the limitation, the self-sacrificing nature of such a role; at the same time he realizes that Morgan is urging him to be a rescuer, an alternative which because it would entail masculine, aggressive action (and the confidence of being able to support Morgan) is not open to him. His dilemma, and the explanation of his passivity, is that he cannot happily resume the old relationship, as Mrs. Moreen would have him do, nor can he conceive of rescuing Morgan and having Morgan, no longer a victim, become absolutely dependent on him. He has suggested and flirted with the latter alternative but he is unable and unwilling to project it in practical terms. Morgan is trying to take their love out of its original context on the assumption that it is independent of context, but, since everything depends on Pemberton, such a change is not possible. Furthermore, it is obvious to Pemberton that the Moreens will not be able to stave off "public exposure" much longer and that disaster will bring about change. Thus he waits "in a queer confusion of yearning and alarm for the catastrophe which was held to hang over the house of Moreen" (471), for which one may read "the house of moreen."

All of the seeing through culminates in the brilliant final scene of the story. Pemberton and Morgan have returned from a walk to discover that the family has been found out by the proprietor of their hotel: they are publicly disgraced. "When Morgan took all this in—and he took it in very quickly—he coloured to the roots of his hair. He had walked from his infancy among difficulties and dangers, but he had never seen a public exposure" (473). The world now knows the Moreens, and Morgan can see this. "Tears of a new and untasted bitterness" come into his eyes, for this, we remember, is *his* family (473). It is a crushing blow for Morgan to have the world a party to his secret knowledge of the fakery of his family. But even he has not measured their depths; there is more seeing through to be done. Mrs.

Moreen asks Pemberton to take Morgan away with him. At first Morgan is overjoyed, distracted from the family humiliation:

> He had a moment of boyish joy, scarcely mitigated by the reflection that with this unexpected consecration of his hope—too sudden and too violent; the turn taken was away from a *good* boy's book—the "escape" was left on their hands. The boyish joy was there an instant, and Pemberton was almost scared at the rush of gratitude and affection that broke through his first abasement. When he stammered "My dear fellow, what do you say to *that?*" how could one not say something enthusiastic? (475)

At this point the meaning of his mother's gesture strikes Morgan (appropriately enough, in the heart). Now that the full identity of his parents has been revealed publicly, now that they are known to be moreen, Morgan is denied whatever inadequate claim to identity he may have had. His parents have no more use for him; they will give him away. Morgan suffers a fatal heart attack, for he has seen through to the fact that without identity there is no basis for life or for love. In the moment before his death Morgan is held by the hands of Pemberton and Mrs. Moreen; at this moment Morgan and Pemberton (or is it Pemberton and Mrs. Moreen?) "look all their dismay into each other's eyes" (475). It is the dismay of the final seeing through, a silent recognition that for Morgan there is nothing.

But it is a dismay and a seeing through that involves Pemberton as well as the Moreen family. During the final scene Pemberton has said nothing to Morgan. He wonders "if he might pretend not to understand" Mrs. Moreen's suggestion, "but everything good gave way to the intensity of Morgan's understanding" (474; in *Longman's* the latter clause reads, "but the idea was painfully complicated by the immediate perception that Morgan had understood"). He feels "almost scared at the rush of gratitude and affection," obliged to answer Morgan's exclamation enthusiastically. His only words come at the moment of Morgan's death, in the form of a medical pronouncement: " 'He couldn't stand it with his weak organ . . . the shock, the whole scene, the violent emotion' " (475).

This final scene has brought matters to a head for Pemberton. He is now being urged by the Moreen family to take away a de-victimized Morgan. And although he is not forced to reject Morgan overtly, it is obvious that he does not want Morgan (he has only wanted Morgan *Moreen*). Pemberton has returned and waited "in a queer confusion of yearning and alarm" for Morgan's death. Let us note that he has waited in a *queer* confusion. For Pemberton, passive, dependent, yet imaged by Morgan as a savior, is in a queer confusion. And it is a measure of how far the Moreen family will go that they would in a sense marry off Morgan to Pemberton. They have been unsuccessful in their attempts to marry off their daughters, Paula and Amy, but here is a chance for them to succeed in their moment of defeat by getting rid of their prize. It is no wonder that Mrs. Moreen rubs her "plump white hands" as she makes the suggestion (474).

Pemberton has indeed poisoned Morgan by his suggestion that Morgan could depend on him, by his failure to be a savior of any kind. Powerless to devise an antidote to his poison, he has waited to see what will happen. And thus when the action of the Moreens causes Morgan's heart attack, Pemberton—still the would-be but inadequate doctor—can offer only a diagnosis. He shares the responsibility for the hopelessness of Morgan's death.

Exactly how much of this Morgan knows James does not spell out for us: he leaves us with the provocative but ambiguous image of Morgan and Pemberton or Pemberton and Mrs. Moreen looking "all their dismay into each other's eyes." We can see through Pemberton; we can see that he has failed Morgan, that he has offered him no encouragement in the last moments of his life. If the look of dismay is to have fullest significance, however, it must involve the total situation of which the Moreens and Pemberton are complementary parts. At this point, I believe, Morgan sees through Pemberton—indeed, all the evidence of the story, his sensitiveness, his devotion to and dependence on Pemberton, his intelligence, points to this. Morgan sees through to the quality of Pemberton's failure, to the fact that there will be no rescue by Pemberton, and no attempt at rescue. It would follow that he sees, too, exactly what his family would do with him. It is the logical last link in the story: Morgan and Pemberton confront each other; and the pupil sees through. James has given us a view of the intricacy and complexity of "*all* the dimensions"; he has carefully wrought his "superpositions of effect."

By seeing into the chaos of self that is his world, Morgan has gained the ultimate vision and has been destroyed by it. Daisy Miller dies not knowing why—Morgan dies knowing precisely why. James closes out his story by telling us what we might expect, that "after the very first" Mr. Moreen took his bereavement "as a man of the world" (475). Pemberton, "after a considerable interval," remembers "the queerness of the Moreens" as "something phantasmagoric, like a prismatic reflexion or a serial novel." "If it were not for a few tangible tokens," writes James, "a lock of Morgan's hair cut by his own hand, and the half-dozen letters received from him when they were disjoined—the whole episode and the figures peopling it would seem too inconsequent for anything but dreamland" (426). The lock of hair and the letters are conventional lover's tokens; that Pemberton assures himself of the reality of the experience by such tokens seems to indicate a desire to remember himself as a lover; it would probably be the most ennobling pose he could reconstruct, though to make himself the hero (or heroine) of the piece he would have to resort to phantasmagoria, to "prismatic reflexion," or perhaps to the techniques of the "serial novel." Blind to the full significance of what they have done, the Moreens and Pemberton thus survive. But the pupil is dead—the pupil who mastered the art and paid the price of seeing through.

"The Pupil": The Education of a Prude

by William Bysshe Stein

It is difficult to reconcile the conventional interpretations of "The Pupil" to James's own vision of the story.

The bitter condemnation of the Moreen troupe, so familiar in current critiques, does not coincide with his treatment of the subject of American Bohemianism in Europe. This univocal approach to theme, in its desperate moralism, ignores, as he puts it in the preface to the New York Edition, the "proportion and perspective" that "contributes to a view of *all* the dimensions." I mean by this that the reader with a self-conscious conscience mediates the meaning of the story through the sensibilities of Pemberton and Morgan Moreen, individually and cumulatively. While the moral intention of this perspective is no doubt admirable, it is nevertheless misguided seriousness. We must see the collective image of the Moreens through, I calculate, three dimensions of aesthetic distance; for James's execution of this work shows him "Addicted to seeing 'through'—one thing through another, accordingly, and still other things through *that*." This narrative mode prohibits our taking the expressed opinion of any single character in the story as the arbitrary standard of the truth of the reality under re-creation. Yet, if one turns to the interpretations in print, he will find the statements of Pemberton and Morgan nakedly presented as vehicles of theme. Let me say at this point that James is concerned with projecting "their moral vibrations"; but this does not necessarily indicate that these impressions of experience are not defiled by too much sensibility. Indeed, in the preface Morgan is compared to "portentous little Hyacinth of *Princess Casamassima,*" who is "tainted to the core . . . with the trick of mental reaction on the things about him and fairly staggering under the appropriations . . . that he owes to the critical spirit." This quite obviously is also the burden of Pemberton.

If I may risk a formulation of how James intends the reader to view

"'The Pupil': The Education of a Prude," by William Bysshe Stein. From the Arizona Quarterly, *XV, no. 1 (Spring, 1959), 13–22. Reprinted by permission of the author and the* Arizona Quarterly.

the "poor and shabby" Moreens, I would say that three definable lenses of aesthetic distance *in the story* reflect the image of their Bohemianism. A fourth, operative but unobtrusive, controls the reader's degree of subjective involvement in the adjudicative function of the first three. In order, James screens the unique flavor of this period of American social history through the various states of sensibility of his central intelligence. He exhibits Pemberton, for instance, in moments of unrehearsed and spontaneous reaction to events. At another time he is presented in mechanical response to concrete occurrences on which occasions we witness his natively conditioned moral reflexes. Finally we view him in acts of perception of incidents in which Morgan is his eyes. But the young boy, even though he is precocious and hypersensitive, is the agent and the victim of "a *good* boy's book" of morality, a code of make-believe honor and dignity. In terms of specific values, this code is connected with "a tradition of self-respect," with "the model one wanted one's family to follow." In it are incorporated an old grandfather of "property" who belongs to "the Bible Society" and is "a good type" along with an aunt, "pure and refined," who disapproves of the Moreens' ways and is likewise "a good type." This "private ideal" is also the product of "a romantic imagination, fed by poetry and history"; for "he would have liked those who 'bore his name' . . . to carry themselves with an air."

This is the sensibility, we must keep in mind, which is constantly at the service of Pemberton. It is arbitrary, pedantic, authoritarian, and imaginary. It is hostile to the reality of the environment in which it is found. But, as James would have us see it, it is a capacity for receptivity that has to be indulged but not necessarily applied to lived experience. Ironically, however, Pemberton begins to share the values of this world of fantasy because these infantile aspirations move in the orbit of his moral universe, which is influenced by the gravitation of Puritanism from his native land. In the preface James makes it quite clear that, with his timidity and unsophistication, it is he who is actually the pupil. His relation to Morgan is one of ludicrous "subjection to *him*," one of "the beguiled, bewildered, defrauded, and unremunerated." And James traces this surrender of adult to childish values to the paradox of an innate Puritanism that European cosmopolitanism intensifies: "He was still young and had not seen much of the world—his English years had been properly arid; therefore the reversed conventions of the Moreens . . . struck him as topsy-turvy. He had encountered nothing like them at Oxford; still less had any such note been struck to his younger American ear during the four years at Yale in which he had richly supposed himself to be reacting against a Puritan strain." The composite sensibility of Pemberton is hardly depicted to arouse the reader's admiration. Rather James subtly unveils it in order to excite our laughter. For though it is a delicate and highly receptive faculty, it is prudish. Its addiction to self-renunciation and self-sacrifice is motivated by a staunch but comical self-righteousness. In this sense, as a scale of dramatic proportion, it is the antithesis of the Bohemian excesses of the Moreens.

Appropriately, then, the fourth dimension of aesthetic distance substantiates, I think, this observation. This is the "through" lens of tone, a narrative ingredient not unfamiliar to the readers of James's prefaces. In this case it is an emotional quality that permeates his treatment of the subject. It may be said to constitute the "atmospheric" character of the story, for, consistent with this reconstitution of a phase of American social history, it is romantic and nostalgic. And, as an a priori condition of the creative act, it determines his preconceptions of the moral timbre of the adult Moreens. They represent for him "the family then of the great unstudied precursors" who boldly invaded Europe in quest of its treasures. They are not, it is significant, to be associated with the modern pilgrims, "the unconscious barbarians." They belong, instead, to the first company of explorers to whom James is sentimentally attached: "They had nothing to do, the poor Moreens, with this dreadful period, any more than I, as occupied and charmed with them, was humiliatingly subject to it; we were, all together, of a better romantic age and faith; we referred ourselves, with our highest complacency, to the classic years of the great Americano-European legend." My evaluation here, of course, can be challenged. As some critics have said, this is patent self-mockery. I will say that it could be if we didn't have *William Wetmore Story and his Friends* to establish the validity of James's feeling on the topic of these early Americans.

As he says in this biography, "We have more things than they, but we have less and less room for them, either in our lives or in our minds; so that even if our taste is superior we have less use for it, and thereby, to our loss, less enjoyment of our relations." With all of their mistakes, their ignorance and presumption, we are indebted to them for "the price they paid." In the humiliation, the frustration, and the shame of the Moreens, James totals such an account for us. At any rate, it is in this light that I view the final scene of the story. The confiscation of the clothes and the defeat of social play entailed are the devices of slapstick comedy, and they are hilarious. True, Morgan's death occurs in the same context, but for a purpose. The two events taken together constitute the climax of Pemberton's education. James seems to say that the European pilgrim is under obligation to bring his sensibilities into free and perceptive relationship with the personal, social, aesthetic, and moral forces of the old world. Only this kind of immersion in experience can bring self-knowledge. Pemberton, with almost feminine fastidiousness, shrinks from this full encounter with truth. Yet, as James argues so often in his novels, too great a refinement of the sensibilities (Morgan and his friend seem to anticipate the dilemma of Lambert Strether in *The Ambassadors*) is self-defeating. And it seems to me that readers of "The Pupil" are too prone to convert the social gaucherie of the Moreens into egregious immorality. James himself, however, generously excuses these excesses: "It is all because they showed us the way, through having first to find it, with more or less comic and tragic going and coming, for themselves. As we turn over the stray, pale testimonies out of which we pick up their history, their simplicities become sacred to us, and their very mistakes acquire a charm. These mistakes are sometimes, verily, great enough to make us wonder what sensibility . . . could flicker in such darkness; then again we see their good faith was what supported them through their tribulations from which we are exempt." In sum, the Moreens in their perhaps too callous social resilience are not wholly admirable, but, on the other hand, neither are they moral criminals. They are simply the earliest victims of the fever of social aspiration that afflicted Americans, great and small, in their first intercourse with European culture. If we scorn them, let us be fair; let us include the self-complacent boor Christopher Newman in *The American*. Though he is a victim of foreign corruption, his inward blindness invites sacrifice.

In this perspective the Moreen clan ought to elicit our pity, though not our compassion. We can reserve this latter feeling for Morgan and Pemberton with their excessive moral vibrations. These two perhaps figure the later development of American sensibility in Europe. The mutual disorientation of their sensibilities argues the need of an intelligent and mature assimilation of the older cultural values, not a fearful, priggish rebellion against them. And this was to come. But in the course of the story James carefully delineates the various stages of Pemberton's revulsion against the behavior of the Moreens, a revulsion that, at its peak, proclaims the resurgence of the Puritan moral fervor that underlay his timid, inhibited quest for identity in the old world. In his first encounter with the Moreens, he immediately labels the father "a man of the world." At this particular moment the epithet has not any definite signification except social manners. But thereafter, as his animosity for him and his family increases, the same epithet is invoked whenever he makes his entry into a scene. But gradually the term evolves into a curse, an anathema of righteous wrath. And at the end of the story, the last phrase as a matter of fact, Pemberton uses it again to support his belief in the immortality of the parents, especially Mr. Moreen. But in a drastic failure of self-insight, he refuses to recognize that it is his reluctant response to the boy's plan of escape that causes Morgan to collapse in despair. James presents this resolution unequivocally in the young pupil's transcendence over the disgrace of his family: "His sense of shame for their common humiliated state had dropped; the case had another side—the thing was to clutch at *that.*" But, unfortunately, he clutches at emptiness, for Pemberton stammers: " 'My dear fellow, what do you say to *that?*' how could one not say something enthusiastic?." This is a fatal betrayal, unexpected as it is. He knew his parents, but he did not know Pemberton's moral involvement in their affairs had become self-protective. Reverting to an atavistic Puritanism, he had to escape the man of the world—the devil—at any cost.

This attack on the integrity of Pemberton may seem to savor of the hostility of other critics towards the parents, but I look upon these disclosures as part of James's comedy of the Americano-European legend. I say this because the extension of "man of the world" leitmotif is also attended by another pattern of adjudicative imagery. This one is initiated in his first attempt to assimilate the bizarre antics of the Moreens into his framework of values: "He had thought himself very sharp that first day in hitting them all off in his mind with the 'cosmopolite' label. Later it seemed feeble and colorless—confessedly helplessly provisional." A little more than a year later this social valuation changes radically. It is now converted into a pompous moral judgment in consonance with his dependence upon the principles of his Puritan conscience: "He had simply given himself away to a band of adventurers. The idea, the word itself, were a romantic horror for him—he had always loved on such safe lines. Later it assumed a more interesting, almost a soothing, sense: it pointed a moral, and Pemberton could enjoy a moral." The nature of this moral is illogical and absurd, but it divulges his surrender to the theology of his forebears: "Oh they were 'respectable,' and that made them more *immondes!*" This French term is fashioned from the biblical attribute of uncleanliness and impurity. It is, as it were, a contemptuous pejorative reserved for the use of the chosen people. By its rhetorical candor, the word shows James in the process of disrobing Pemberton of all tolerance, of all humanity. Hence it is no great surprise that at a later time this moral superiority becomes a habit, comically accentuated by his conversations with Morgan about his parents: "the real problem came up—the problem of how far it was excusable to discuss the *turpitude* of parents with a child of twelve, of thirteen, of fourteen." (italics mine) This sequence of the boy's age indicates how obsessive the tutor's concern with the evilness of the Moreens' social mores had become. Their behavior was no longer a matter of cosmopolitan eccentricity; it now was a manifestation of depravity, of inherent baseness, of original sin. Moreover, what they did was indistinguishable from European culture, its power to corrupt the innocent. The situation which illuminates this point also bares Pemberton's inability to adapt himself to a familial Bohemianism as innocuous as a handshake: "She squeezed forward in her dressing-gown, and he received her in his own, between his bath-tub and his bed. He had been tolerably schooled by this time to the 'foreign ways' of his hosts." The marshalling of all this indelicate imagery, though it is part of the setting, emphasizes the state of Pemberton's consciousness, its prudishness, its sin-centeredness. In the final analysis it likewise explains his servitude to the private ideal of Morgan whose inveterate condemnation of his family pivots on the colloquial usage of beastly: "They're so beastly worldly." The repetition of this metaphor impinges upon the mind of the tutor in its animalistic connotations, leading him to associate the Moreens with a "view of life, dim and confused and instinctive, like that of clever colour-blind animals." From another angle of vision, of course, we see in operation here James's addiction to seeing one thing through another and still another. This is to say that we observe here an image of the Moreens subtly filtered through the boy's ingenuous code, through his tutor's impression of it, and finally through the sin-screening conscience of the latter. Surely, we cannot take this composite impression of the Moreens as any more than a distorted reflection of reality—the comic adumbration of an unappreciative American pilgrim in Europe.

In contrast with Pemberton's moralizing propensities, it is interesting to note his spontaneous reactions to the behavior of his employers. At the beginning of their association he immediately senses their piquant difference from conventional people, their lack of inhibition, their delight in life: "He yet when he first applied it [the cosmopolite label] felt a glow of joy—for an instructor he was still empirical—rise from the apprehension that living with them would really be to see life. Their sociable strangeness was an imitation of that—their chatter of tongues, their gaiety and good humor, their infinite dawdling . . . , their French, their Italian and, cropping up in the foreign fluencies, their cold tough slices of American." Even several years later he is still able to muster some admiration for them, and mind you, despite Morgan's insidious deprecations: "They continued to 'chivey,' as Morgan called it, and in due time became aware of a variety of reasons for preceding them to Venice. They mentioned a great many of them—*they were always strikingly frank* and had the brightest friendly chatter, at the late foreign breakfast in especial, before the ladies had made up their faces, when they leaned their arms on the table, had something to follow the *demi-tasse,* and, in the heat of familiar discussion as what they 'really ought' to do, fell into the languages in which they could *tutoyer*. Even Pemberton liked them then." (italics mine) In these pictures James seeks to warn the reader that he must maintain "proportion and perspective" in regard to these "candid children of the West." However incongruous and incredible their actions may appear to Pemberton, they do not deliberately attempt to deceive the tutor. They are incapable of this sort of deception. Their social deceit is another thing. They are forced into it by their preposterous ambitions and by the society in which they move. They are explorers and illuminators. Their mistakes prepare for the easier initiation of later generations of Americans in Europe. Pemberton's ambivalence in this situation is derived from his inability to reconcile their personal candor to their manneristic affectations. This is the inward conflict that, from the standpoint of James's narrative execution, is designed to clarify his function in the story. He is its comic center.

Ultimately, in his loss of generosity and tolerance, he is converted into a scapegoat. He is sacrificed on the cross of his dogmatic seriousness. And, paradoxically, it is Morgan who thus victimizes him. As I have argued, Pemberton is the dupe of a fanciful code of respectability, one which Morgan reiterates because he instinctively knows that this is his major appeal to the tutor. In this way he converts the latter into "the hero" of his fantasy world. This turn of events is not unusual in the Jamesian story. It simply is a version of the comedy of sensibility which is implicit in even his most serious works. For, surely, one facet of the ambiguity of his fiction lies in the ostensible rapport of individuals in terms of sensibility; yet we discover, as in the case of Madame de Vionnet–Lambert Strether relationship, that the seeming equipoise of mutual interests is effected by the excessive sensibility of one of the characters. The failure to perceive this incongruity generates the pathos of defeat in which so many of James's characters find themselves. In "The Pupil" we can call this outcome the failure of education. The prude, because he attempts to write the book of life in the idiom of his own subjective life, ends up holding an untranslatable form of experience. This is Pemberton's fate: "Indeed the whole mystic volume in which the boy had been amateurishly bound demanded some practice in translation. Today, after a considerable interval, there is something phantasmagoric, like a prismatic reflexion or a serial novel, in Pemberton's memory of the queerness of the Moreens." In this single passage James sums up, not only the topic of the tutor's self-deception, but his mode of dramatizing this experience.

James's "The Real Thing": Three Levels of Meaning

by Earle Labor

Despite its popularity in the classroom (it is perhaps the most anthologized of all Henry James's stories), "The Real Thing" continues to be read as a little masterpiece which, according to Clifton Fadiman, "expresses amusingly (and no more than that) the old truth that art is a *transformation* of reality, not a mere reflection of the thing itself."[1] Without commenting upon Mr. Fadiman's curious sense of humor, I should like to demonstrate that James's theme—an "exquisite" question, as he put it—includes considerably "more than that."

It should be evident that, were the central meaning of "The Real Thing" no more than an esthetic cliché, the question that struck James's sensibility could hardly have been an exquisite one. An intelligence so fine seldom concerned itself with platitudes. It is of course James's remarkable fusion of the simple and the complex, the explicit and the subtle, that makes "The Real Thing" so admirably suited to the literary and critical initiation of the college student. Not only does James provide a commentary upon the nature of art (his theme obviously applies to writing as well as to painting); his story is also an excellent illustration of the thing itself. Like his painter-narrator, the author has, through "the alchemy of art," transformed a rather

---

"James's 'The Real Thing': Three Levels of Meaning," by Earle Labor. From College English, *XXIII (February, 1962), 376–78. Reprinted by permission of the author and the National Council of Teachers of English.*

[1] "A Note on The Real Thing," *The Short Stories of Henry James* (New York, 1945), p. 217. Several critics have gone beyond Fadiman's superficial reading of this story; especially noteworthy are the following: William F. Marquardt, "A Practical Approach to *The Real Thing* by Henry James," *English "A" Analyst* (Northwestern University), no. 14 (June 13, 1949); Quentin Anderson, ed., *Henry James: Selected Short Stories* (New York, 1957), pp. vii–ix; and Walter F. Wright, "The Real Thing," *Research Studies of the State College of Washington,* XXV (March, 1957), 85–90. Also, see Edward Stone, ed., *Henry James: Seven Stories and Studies* (New York, 1961), pp. 131–41, 309; and Maurice Beebe and William T. Stafford, "Criticism of Henry James: A Selected Checklist with an Index to Studies of Separate Works," *Modern Fiction Studies,* III (Spring, 1957), 91.

trivial episode involving two dull social has-beens, the Monarchs, and a couple of grubby nobodies, Miss Churm and Oronte, into a work of art that is rich with universality and "felt life." From this standpoint, the story is itself "the real thing," though I doubt that James intended to be so "clever" about his title.

From a more serious point of view, there are three major thematic levels in "The Real Thing": (1) the social, (2) the esthetic, and (3) the moral. About (1) James is quite explicit: socially speaking, Major and Mrs. Monarch have been and still are the real thing; they are, as the porter's wife immediately informs us, "a gentleman and a lady." They are neither "celebrities" nor "personalities," and they have lost their money; but they have retained the essential quality that makes them what they are: their manners. Furthermore, "They weren't superficial." And their marriage (*the* social institution) "had no weak spot. It was a real marriage . . . a nut for pessimists to crack."

Unhappily, as the narrator complains, the real thing for society is "the wrong thing" for art. In the "deceptive atmosphere of art even the highest respectability may fail of being plastic." In other words, the real thing for the artist must be "the ideal thing." On a second and higher level of meaning, then, the real thing—esthetically—is the creative imagination of the artist himself. (1) cannot accommodate itself to (2), nor vice versa. It is from the conflict between these two levels of meaning that the tension within the story partially derives. The Monarchs prove to be utterly intractable for the artist's purposes. The painter's foolish attempt to amalgamate these incompatible elements almost ruins his project and, worse, perhaps irreparably mars his creative talent, if we are to accept the word of his esthetic conscience, Jack Hawley.

But are we to accept Hawley's judgment? I think we must—at least from the purely esthetic viewpoint. Our narrator makes it fairly clear that his friend's critical insights are trustworthy: ". . . he was always of such good counsel. He painted badly himself, but there was no one like him for putting his finger on the place." Hawley perceives almost immediately that if the painter is to preserve his artistic integrity the Monarchs must be got rid of: " 'Ce sont des gens qu'il faut mettre à la porte.' " Notwithstanding his critical incisiveness, however, Jack Hawley is heartless. And this is the key to the third level of meaning in the story, a meaning that James skillfully withholds until his concluding sentence—a meaning so deftly manipulated that it has apparently been overlooked by most of James's critics.

Following his friend's sound advice, the painter dismisses the pathetically inept Monarchs, who, according to Hawley, "did me a permanent harm, got me into false ways." Then he concludes with this enigmatic qualification: "If it be true I'm content to have paid the price—for the memory." An astounding concession for any artist to make! In essence, the narrator admits that he has been willing to sacrifice something of the artist's most precious gift, his creative talent, for something else termed vaguely as "the memory."

In order to determine exactly what the painter (and James) means by this, we must carefully re-examine the story. That the narrator, not the Monarchs, is James's central character is patent. It is he who undergoes the most subtle and dynamic inner change during the course of the narrative. The change is manifested primarily in his attitude toward the Monarchs. At first he views them from the commercial perspective: "Sitters my visitors in this case proved to be; but not in the sense I should have preferred"—i.e., the *commercial* sense. When Major Monarch confesses, "We should like to make it pay," the painter immediately supposes that he means "pay the artist." Significantly, the narrator also looks at his art chiefly as a means "to perpetuate my fame" and "to make my fortune." Upon discovering that the Monarchs have no useful purpose in this scheme, he regards them with detached, even slightly cruel, amusement: "I had seized their type—I had already settled what I would do with it. Something that wouldn't absolutely have pleased them, I afterwards reflected." When he good-naturedly attempts to take their point of view, he cannot help "appraising physically, as if they were animals on hire. . . ." The metaphor recurs when Mrs. Monarch is put "through her paces before him," like a prize mare. The extent of the painter's sympathy for her humiliating gesture is that he abstains from applauding. And, when she bursts into tears, he merely reassures her politely.

Compare this opening scene with the final one in which the Monarchs, stripped of everything but the wistful desire not to starve, voluntarily assume the services of menials. Here, the tears are those, not of Mrs. Monarch, but of the painter himself: "When it came over me, the latent eloquence of what they were doing, I confess that my drawing was blurred for a moment—the picture swam." His attitude has changed radically from what it was at the beginning of the story. He is now involved with mankind. Though such involvement may have blurred his esthetic perspective, it has sharpened his moral insight; if he has lost something as an artist, he has gained infinitely more as a man. From his painful experience with the Monarchs James's narrator emerges with a finer understanding of the human situation and with a new awareness of what constitutes "the real thing" in human relationships: compassion.

This is the third and highest level of meaning in James's title, and it is this alone that justifies the artist's willingness to renounce his talent. Paradoxically, Henry James implies that only through such an attitude may the artist achieve true greatness. As he says in his preface to *The Portrait of a Lady,* it is, after all, the "enveloping air of the artist's humanity—which gives the last touch to the worth of the work. . . ." And it is the latent moral value of the painter's "memory" which gives the last exquisite touch to the worth of "The Real Thing."

Narrative Irony in Henry James' "The Real Thing"

by David Toor

A great part of the critical discussion about Henry James' story "The Real Thing" has been concerned with the artistic theory that is supposedly developed in the tale; that is, that the chief irony of the story rests in the conclusion of the painter-narrator that the represented subject is more effective for the artist than the real. No critic I have encountered has examined the story in terms of one of James' favorite devices, the unreliable narrator.

In *Daisy Miller,* for instance, Winterbourne evolves as the central character in his final awareness of what Daisy is all about—and it is through his perceptions that we see the action and learn what he does, adding a depth to our understanding of what he and others have misunderstood about the girl. The device is more clearly used in *What Maisie Knew,* with the ironic center of that novel focussed on the generally inaccurate perceptions of the little girl.

More subtle, and seldom recognized, is the painter-narrator of "The Liar," who, it turns out, is a much more malicious liar than the supposed title character, Colonel Capadose. James insists on this irony of the story by assigning the name "Oliver Lyon" to the real liar of the piece.

Turning to "The Real Thing" with "The Liar" fresh in memory, we can recognize a very important relationship in the question of how much we are to trust the narrators. This leads to the equally important question: How seriously, then, are we to take the esthetic theory advanced by the unnamed "I" of the tale? If doubt can be cast on the objectivity and validity of the narrator's perceptions, then we can doubt what seems to be his artistic theory—and possibly what critics have often considered to be James' idea about the real thing.

"Narrative Irony in Henry James' 'The Real Thing,'" by David Toor. From The University Review, *XXIV (December, 1967), 95–99. Reprinted by permission of the author and* The University Review.

James gives little hint to this ironic aspect of the story in his comments in *The Notebooks*.[1] The story came from an anecdote related by his friend, the painter George Du Maurier, concerning a couple very much like the Monarchs. The idea of inserting an esthetic theory came after the germ of the story, and he does hint at a possible twist in his depiction of the narrator: "He is willing to give them [the couple] a trial. Make it out that *he* himself is on trial—he is young and 'rising,' but he has still his golden spurs to win." [2]

The point I raise here is that it is indeed a trial for the artist, and that he fails it.

"The Real Thing" tells of a destitute couple, Major and Mrs. Monarch, approaching the narrator for work as models. They have heard he has a large project coming up, illustrating the writings of "the rarest of the novelists . . . long neglected by the multitudinous vulgar and dearly prized by the attentive. . . ." [3] (Let us not ignore the deliberate choice of the word "attentive" here.) The Monarchs proffer themselves as suitable models for such an undertaking, and the painter agrees to try them. They don't work out, and the narrator uses his other models, two coarse and unrefined individuals, Miss Churm and Oronte, and eventually sends the Monarchs off. As I've said, most of the critics concern themselves with the problem apparently illustrated here: the fake, or representation of the object, is often more real for the artist's purposes than the real thing, as the Monarchs are quite real and Miss Churm and Oronte obviously are not.

James was concerned with the length of his story—he had to keep it reasonably short for the publications he had in mind for it, to choose the telling and most significant details: "But in how tremendously few words I must do it. This is a lesson—a *magnificent* lesson—if I'm to do a good many. Something as admirably compact and *selected* as Maupassant." [4] It is in the cumulative effect of the selected details that we must look for the deeper irony of "The Real Thing." In a story as controlledly compact as this, James could introduce nothing extraneous.

The conception of the Monarchs is frequently on the level of farce —rather unreal characters in a real situation, but they are types that James had seen often and generally disliked. "Stupid" he called them

[1] *The Notebooks of Henry James,* ed. F. O. Matthiessen and Kenneth B. Murdock (New York, 1947), pp. 102–5.

[2] *Notebooks,* p. 103.

[3] *The Short Stories of Henry James,* ed. Clifton Fadiman (New York, 1945), p. 195. All citations from "The Real Thing" refer to this edition.

[4] *Notebooks,* p. 104.

in working them out.[5] They are a ridiculous couple—and we don't have to rely altogether on the narrator's telling this to us. It is a pitiable situation, but no matter how the narrator is amused at the couple, there are things which extend their plight beyond the level of mere farce. They did not first come to the painter "to sit"—they had tried other things, and modeling was their last resort.

There is a depth in the Major that the painter is reluctant to admit, but that is made clear in his words and actions. It is in the conversations that are reported, not in the observations of the narrator on the couple, that the other side to the distastefulness of the situation becomes most clear. "It's awfully hard—we've tried everything." (p. 196) As the Major makes this difficult confession to the painter, his wife sits crying. "There isn't a confounded job I haven't applied for—waited for—prayed for. You can fancy we'd be pretty bad first. . . . I'd be *anything*—I'm strong; a messenger or a coalheaver." (p. 197)

Again, they are a ridiculous pair, but unquestionably the real thing. The irony of both the title and the story is intensified in our knowledge of this fact, and much more in the more subtly ironic fact that the painter, in spite of his ambitions and protestations, is not the real thing. But the Monarchs are not where we find the meaning of the story. For that we must focus most directly on the narrator.

James recognized the necessity of art to transcend life—that the artist selects and changes and recreates life—but if a difficulty arises in translating the real into the artificial, the possibility must not be overlooked that it is the artist and not the object at fault. In "The Real Thing," the narrator justifies himself for his failure with the Monarchs—shifting the blame to them.

One of his earliest reactions to the presence of the Monarchs in his studio illustrates much concerning his attitude towards them: "I liked them—I felt, quite as their friends must have done—they were so simple; and I had no objection to them if they would suit. But somehow with all their perfections I didn't easily believe in them. After all they were amateurs, and the ruling passion of my life was the detestation of the amateur. Combined with this was another perversity—an innate preference for the represented subject over the real one: the defect of the real one was so apt to be a lack of representation. I like things that appeared; then one was sure." (p. 194) We cannot help but question these perceptions—his perversities. It is not unreasonable to accuse the artist possessed of such perceptions of superficiality.

He is admittedly a hack, turning out illustrations "in black-and-white, for magazines, for storybooks, for sketches of contemporary life." (p. 189) Yet his aspirations seem to go beyond this work. He looks

[5] *Notebooks*, p. 103.

forward to achieving more, specifically as "a great painter of portraits." But it is in an offhand way that he tells of his ambitions, and they never seem to be concerned with the production of art for its own rewards.

Quite early in the story, just at the first appearance of the Monarchs, he tells us of his ambitions. We learn that he has been doing illustrations and that he often used models for the work: "These things are true, but it was not less true—I may confess it now; whether because the aspiration was to lead to everything or to nothing I leave the reader to guess—that I couldn't get the honours, to say nothing of the emoluments, of a greater painter of portraits out of my head. My 'illustrations' were my pot-boilers; I looked to a different branch of art far and away the most interesting it had always seemed to me—to perpetuate my fame. There was no shame in looking to it also to make my fortune." (p. 189)

The major concerns, as he tells us here, are "honours," "emoluments," and the desire to "perpetuate my fame." The ambiguity of the parenthetical remark, leaving the reader to guess whether it "was to lead to everything or to nothing," seems another hint to the "attentive" reader that there is more to the story than is at first apparent.

This ambition, his desire to be that "great painter of portraits," seems to be in direct conflict with his abilities as demonstrated in the story. He is totally unequipped to handle either of the Monarchs, the real things. When he tries to paint the lady, it doesn't work out. "But after a little skirmishing I began to find her too insurmountably stiff; do what I would with it my drawing looked like a photograph or a copy of a photograph. Her figure had no variety of expression—she herself had no sense of variety. You may say that this was my business, and was only a question of placing her." (p. 201)

He anticipates our objection, but it is much more than a question of his merely placing her. It was certainly his business, as it is the business of any artist, to take the object, whatever it is, and recreate through what the narrator himself calls "the alchemy of art." Whether the object be a vase of flowers, a bowl of fruit, or Mrs. Monarch, that *is* his business. If he can't do it, why must the fault rest with the material and not with the sensitivity of the artist? He has little trouble dealing with Miss Churm. It isn't strange, for she is very much like him: "After I had drawn Mrs. Monarch a dozen times I felt surer even than before that the value of such a model as Miss Churm resided precisely in the fact that she had no positive stamp, combined of course with the other fact that what she did have was a curious and inexplicable talent for imitation." (p. 202)

In a way this is precisely what the narrator possesses, a "talent for imitation." Mrs. Monarch, in her rather simple-minded innocence, recognizes this immediately: "Now the drawings you make from *us*, they look exactly like us." (p. 206) The similarity of the painter to Miss Churm is underlined in her reaction to his request that she serve tea to the Monarchs. "She had tried intonations—as if she too wished to pass for the real thing." (p. 204)

There is a subtlety in his relation to the Monarchs that points out what might almost be conceived of as a kind of jealousy on the artist's part. What happens in his portrayals of the Monarchs is another indication of his inability to cope with what he considers the real thing. He makes giants of them; their size is beyond control in his drawings. His comment says more than he intends: "Arrange as I would and take the precautions I would, she always came out, in my pictures, too tall—landing me in the dilemma of having represented a fascinating woman as seven feet high, which (out of respect perhaps to my own very much scantier inches) was far from my idea of such a personage." (p. 201)

One of the primary—and most subtle—motivations in the story is to bring about what is finally demonstrated in the final scene of the Monarchs in the story—their serving him in the capacity of menials. In a way this is what he has been after through the story, to bring them down a few pegs, almost to find a scapegoat for what he somehow must recognize as his own inadequacies.

We see this in his reaction to what he takes to be Mrs. Monarch's attitude towards him—in his attempt to ridicule her pretensions: "She wished it to remain clear that she and the Major were employed, not cultivated, and if she approved of me as a superior, who could be kept in his place, she never thought me quite good enough for an equal." (p. 201)

He is amused by the Monarchs, he tells us, and he takes clear pleasure in viewing their growing discomfiture. He enjoys manipulating them, placing them in awkward situations, watching their encounters with Miss Churm and Oronte. Again, his similarities to Miss Churm are underlined when he muses, "they must have felt—in the air—that she was amused at them, secretly derisive of their ever knowing how." (p. 203)

After trying them and finding them unsuitable—after doing more, after bringing them to the level of servants, he finally gives them some money and sends them off, but he tells us that he has learned a lot from them, and in the last sentence of the story gives us a glimpse into what he really has become. The ambiguity of the earlier remark—leaving the reader to guess whether he ever achieved his ambition—is less uncertain when looked at in the context of the closing self-excuse of those last sentences. He sends them off and gets the remaining books of the series to illustrate, "but my friend Hawley repeats that Major and Mrs. Monarch did me a permanent harm, got me into false ways. If it be true I'm content to have paid the price—for the memory." (p. 215) The "permanent harm" was not done by the Monarchs—it is convenient, I think, that he have someone or something to blame.

There are few references to the narrator's friends in the story, but those are significant. It is Jack Hawley's opinion with which the story closes, and we may also question his reliability. Hawley is another painter who is in agreement with the narrator about the Monarchs—and the narrator tells us that Hawley is a better critic than painter: "He painted badly himself, but there was no one like him for putting his finger on the place. He had been absent from England for a year; he had been somewhere—I don't remember where—to get a fresh eye. I was in a good deal of dread of any such organ, but we were old friends." (p. 208)

When Hawley sees what the narrator has been doing in a drawing of the Monarchs, he reacts strongly: "I asked if he didn't think it good, and he replied that it struck him as execrable, given the sort of thing I had always represented myself to him as wishing to arrive at." (p. 209)

Hawley's observation, "Well, there's a big hole somewhere," is indicative. When he can't comment any more conclusively than that, he too blames the models. In his artistic French he tells the narrator: "Ce sont des gen qu'il faut mettre à la porte." (p. 209)

We don't know whether to trust Hawley—the narrator sees that the paintings of the Monarchs are indeed "execrable," but he takes Hawley's word for it that the models and not the artist are at fault. It is quite possible that Hawley's mere friendship with the narrator could make his opinions suspect. I mention this possibility because of another one of those little *"selected"* details that James tosses into the story.

There is a single reference to some of the narrator's other friends, or former friends. In an aside in which he attempts to describe his own theory of art, the narrator once again tells us more about himself than he intends:

> I adored variety and range, I cherished human accidents, the illustrative note; I wanted to characterize closely, and the thing in the world I most hated was the danger of being ridden by a type. I had quarrelled with some of my friends about it; I had parted company with them for maintaining that one *had* to be, and that if the type was beautiful—witness Raphael and Leonardo—the servitude was only a gain. I was neither Leonardo nor Raphael—I might only be a presumptuous young modern searcher; but I held that everything was to be sacrificed sooner than character. When they claimed that the obsessional form could easily *be* character, I retorted, perhaps superficially, "Whose?" It couldn't be everybody's—it might end in being nobody's. (p. 202)

We learn from this passage that this "young modern searcher," working in a field in which both Raphael and Leonardo excelled, distrusts them as masters. He will not be "ridden by a type," admitting magnanimously that he was "neither Raphael or Leonardo." On the basis of these arguments he had parted with his friends—the only one remaining is Hawley who obviously doesn't disagree too strongly with the narrator. The "variety and range" that the painter so admires will come, he fails to realize, not from any type or any model, but from the artist himself. He will seek and find in himself all the variety and range and truth that he needs—providing it is there in the artist to be found in the first place.

It is the narrator who lacks—it is the painter who is not the real thing, and all his argument (after the fact), that the Monarchs were impossible for him to use proclaims not so much a valid artistic theory, but an implicit admission of failure on his part that he is not fully ready to make overtly. Thus in the end we see the irony and the subtlety implied in the title of the story.

Henry James' "The Figure in the Carpet": What is Critical Responsiveness?

by Seymour Lainoff

With the exception of "The Turn of the Screw," perhaps no story by Henry James has provoked such diversity of opinion as his satirical fable "The Figure in the Carpet" (1896). Some readers have stated that James here reveals a troubled conscience, perhaps about his own lack of clarity or his viability as a popular author;[1] others, that the story satirizes supersubtle authors.[2] A directly opposite idea, more current, is that the story advocates a more rigorous application of critical methods.[3] All these views seem inadequate. Of written comments on the story, only one I have seen seems to get at its central theme. Quentin Anderson, in *The American Henry James,* correctly perceives that the critical failure of the narrator and his friends does not lie in Vereker's lack of clarity or in some cognitive inability or laziness of their own, but in their failure as human beings, in their inadequate responses to life. Like John Marcher in "The Beast in the Jungle," they are unawakened, therefore ungiving, or like the narrator in "The Aspern

"Henry James' 'The Figure in the Carpet': What is Critical Responsiveness?" by Seymour Lainoff. From Boston University Studies in English, *V (Summer, 1961), 122–28.*

[1] R. P. Blackmur writes ("In the Country of the Blue," in *Critiques and Essays on Modern Fiction, 1920–51,* ed. J. W. Aldridge [New York: Ronald Press, 1952], p. 313): "It is rather like Kafka, manqué, the exasperation of the mystery without the presence of the mystery, or a troubled conscience without any evidence of guilt"; Michael Swan comments (*Henry James* [New York: Roy, 1952], p. 87): "I have suggested that when James wrote his story called *The Figures* [sic] *in the Carpet,* he was revealing his own uncertainty that his work had any more meaning than what was obvious."

[2] P. D. Wesbrook writes ("The Supersubtle Fry," in *Nineteenth-Century Fiction,* VIII [1953], p. 138): "Both on the surface and in its implications the fable is a warning to the critics not to take a self-important author too seriously. . . . The critics in the story are mere dupes; the novelist is a poseur, a fraud."

[3] F. O. Matthiessen states (James, *Stories of Writers and Artists* [New York: New Directions, 1956], p. 7): "James' title has given a phrase to the close textual criticism which he helped to inaugurate."

Papers," they are greedy and overly pragmatic. Because they cannot respond to life satisfactorily, they cannot respond to literature. As Anderson writes: "The critics in *The Figure in the Carpet* . . . have before them an authentically great novelist, whose intention they cannot discover because they have no power to love." [4] I wish to enlarge upon Anderson's comments, differ with them as they pertain to Corvick and Gwendolen Erme, and relate more closely James' characters to the riddle at the center of the story.

If we retain the idea that the narrator and his friends are, on the whole, spiritually inauthentic, the themes of an otherwise puzzling story become clear. First, Hugh Vereker's subtlety as a novelist does not stem from a wilful attempt to confuse, but from his subtle knowledge of life. And, second, the story indicates that no amount of critical finesse can get as much out of a novel as a selfless and affectionate reading, one in which the reader manifests, in James' phrase, a "sense of life."

The first-person narrator, who remains nameless, accepts the task of reviewing Hugh Vereker's latest novel before its date of publication. With the review he hopes to enhance his own reputation: "This was his new novel, an advance copy, and whatever much or little it should do for his reputation I was clear on the spot as to what it should do for mine." The young man's motive for reading the novel is to promote himself. His review, unfortunately, does not meet with the approval of the novelist. Vereker, before learning of the identity of the reviewer, dismisses the review in the narrator's presence as the "usual twaddle." Later, to amend the social blunder he now knows he has committed, Vereker takes the younger man into his confidence. He informs the critic that a pattern exists in his fiction, a figure in the carpet no one has yet detected; the young critic, therefore, he suggests, should not regard the shortcomings of the published review with too much chagrin. The critic has missed the mark, but so has everyone else. The narrator, intrigued by the riddle Vereker has posed him, persists in believing that the pattern or figure consists of some secret formula, although Vereker makes it plain that the figure is the *life* of the work itself, "the passion of his passion":

> I scratched my head. "Is it something in the style or something in the thought? An element of form or an element of feeling?"
>
> He indulgently shook my hand again, and I felt my questions to be crude and my distinctions pitiful. "Good-night, my dear boy—don't bother about it. After all, you do like a fellow."
>
> "And a little intelligence might spoil it?" I still detained him.
>
> He hesitated. "Well, you've got a heart in your body. Is that an element

[4] (New Brunswick: Rutgers University Press, 1957), pp. 148–49.

> of form or an element of feeling? What I contend that nobody has ever mentioned in my work is the organ of life."
>
> "I see—it's some idea *about* life, some sort of philosophy. Unless it be," I added with the eagerness of a thought perhaps still happier, "some kind of game you're up to with your style, something you're after in the language." (pp. 233–34)[5]

The narrator persists in his quest to discover the meaning of Vereker's work; but he is thwarted, James implies, both by his literary and spiritual aridity. He belongs to a clicque of writers given to much lucubration, but possessing an undernourished store of feeling; Vereker calls them "little demons of subtlety." Their chief literary organ is significantly called *The Middle*; Gwendolen Erme, Corvick's fiancée, has written a barren three-volume novel, *Deep Down*, "a desert in which she had lost herself, but in which too she had dug a wonderful hole in the sand—a cavity out of which Corvick had still more remarkably pulled her." The narrator tends to judge others by their "cleverness," a criterion inadequate for judging Vereker. The redeeming quality in his relationship with Vereker is that he likes the novelist personally, a fact Vereker recognizes in the dialogue I have quoted. He continues to like Vereker after he has lost his taste for the author's works through overanalysis. At one point he says: "Not only had I lost the books, but I had lost the man himself: they and their author had been alike spoiled for me. I knew too which was the loss I most regretted. I had taken to the man still more than I had ever taken to the books."

The narrator's too-intent search for meaning defeats its own purpose; since he is not interested in the work itself so much as in the prize awaiting him at the conclusion of his research, the work eludes him. His all-too-practical approach to literature is reflected in the selfishness of his private life as well. Witness his disapproval of his brother's complete and selfless devotion to the study of painting in Munich; his reluctance to take the time to nurse that same brother, grown ill, back to health; his considering marriage to the widowed Gwendolen only so that he might possess the secret revealed to her by Corvick; and his malice toward Drayton Deane, expressed in the closing lines of the story: "I may say that to-day as victims of unappeased desire there isn't a pin to choose between us. The poor man's state is almost my consolation; there are really moments when I feel it to be quite my revenge."

This continued hesitancy to assume the responsibilities of love and friendship stems, for the most part, from his fear that such responsi-

[5] Page references for "The Figure in the Carpet" are to the New York Edition of Henry James, Vol. xv (New York: Charles Scribner's Sons, 1909).

bilities would somehow interfere with his bringing his quest to a successful close. His hesitancy is ironic, for it is only through the willing assumption of these responsibilities that he can achieve his purpose. In his abstract quest for meaning, he relinquishes that which gives life (and literature) its concrete meanings. James interestingly allies the pragmatic and the abstract; since the narrator's quest is purely self-promoting in purpose, it misses the concrete realities of Vereker's work. Vereker had described his figure in the carpet thus: " 'The thing's as concrete there as a bird in a cage, a bait on a hook, a piece of cheese in a mouse-trap. It's stuck into every volume as your foot is stuck into your shoe. It governs every line, it chooses every word, it dots every i, it places every comma' " (p. 233).

James' belief that good art and the appreciation of art should be as concretely rich as life itself is expressed, incidentally, at several points in *The Scenic Art,* a collection of his dramatic criticism. He writes of the art of Mme. Plessy of the Théâtre Français as follows: "When I think of all the experience, the observation, the reflection, the contact with life and art which are summed up in such a mellow maturity of skill, I am struck with a kind of veneration." [6] He cites the statement of an old playgoer he overheard after a memorable performance: "I caught an echo of my impressions from one of them the other evening, when, as the curtain fell on Bressant and Plessy [of the Théâtre Français], he murmured ecstatically to his neighbor, 'Quelle connaissance de la scène . . . et de la vie!' " [7] He mentions as the "largest quality" in Dumas *fils* "his immense concern about life—his sense of human character and human fate as commanding and controllable things." [8]

Quentin Anderson seems to place Corvick and his fiancée, Miss Erme, in the same limbo of nonfulfillment as the narrator. He writes: "Corvick, whose name suggests a bird acquisitive of bright and shining objects, is said to have found the 'figure.' What he has found is an image, or inversion, which reflects his greedy self. His death and the death of his wife promptly ensue, and these are emblematic deaths." [9] I wish to suggest, however, that Corvick is the critical hero of the tale. At first caught in the same web of meaningless analysis as the narrator and Miss Erme, he breaks through to win his critical redemption. True, Corvick is mercenary, a fact evidenced by his waiting with Miss Erme for her rich mother to die before they should wed. But several of Corvick's good qualities are apparent from the beginning. The narrator describes him thus: "He had done more things than I, and

[6] Ed. Allan Wade (New York: Hill and Wang, 1957), p. 50.
[7] *The Scenic Art,* p. 7.
[8] *The Scenic Art,* p. 277.
[9] Anderson, *The American Henry James,* p. 149.

earned more pence, though there were chances for cleverness I thought he sometimes missed." That the narrator thinks Corvick has missed some chances for "cleverness" is an indirect compliment to him. Furthermore, Vereker thinks that Corvick's relationship with Miss Erme might provide Corvick with the key to the novelist's mystery; a love-relationship might teach Corvick to grasp the *feeling* of a work:

> Vereker seemed struck with this. "Do you mean they're to be married?"
> "I dare say that's what it will come to."
> "That may help them," he conceded, "but we must give them time!" (p. 240)

In addition, Corvick, like Vereker, is dissatisfied with the narrator's review; he feels it has missed some essence in Vereker. Above all, what particularly characterizes Corvick, beyond his crassness, is his actual devotion to literature. At several points, the narrator cites Corvick's enthusiasm for art. He states, for instance: "I was frankly struck with my colleague's power to excite himself over a question of art. He'd call it letters, he'd call it life, but it was all one thing."

This enthusiasm for literature leads to the act that liberates Corvick. Corvick abandons a venture that would net him much money in order to hurry to Rapallo, where Vereker is staying because of his wife's poor health, and to announce his discovery. "He had thrown up his commission, he had thrown up his book, he had thrown up everything but the instant need to hurry to Rapallo, on the Genoese shore, where Vereker was making a stay." Vereker receives Corvick wholeheartedly. What the discovery is remains unrevealed. The act itself is Corvick's redemption, the compulsion itself rather than the contents of the discovery; for, in this "significant fable," as James called it, the motive for a behavior determines the value of a behavior. No action has value except in relation to the spirit with which it is performed.

That James intended to separate Corvick in spirit from the narrator, to make Corvick the critical hero, is apparent from his *Notebooks*. James revised his original notion that Vereker should die before any revelation comes to Corvick in order that the validity of Corvick's discovery might be insured. In October 1895 James wrote of the tale in the making as follows:

> Two little things, in relation to this, occur to me. One is the importance of my being *sure* the disclosure has been made to the wife by her 1st husband. The other is the importance of *his* having been sure he had got hold of the right thing. The only way for this would be to have him submit his idea to the Author himself. To this end the Author's death would have *not* to precede his discovery.[10]

[10] *The Notebooks of Henry James,* ed. F. O. Matthiessen and Kenneth B. Murdock (New York: Oxford Univ. Press, 1955), p. 223.

On the strength of his discovery, Corvick decides to marry Gwendolen with no further delay; but he is to die shortly thereafter. His sudden death can be interpreted not so much as emblematic of his spiritual decline, as Anderson suggests, but rather as an immolation. Like May Bartram and Milly Theale, though less significantly, he bears to his grave a secret of existence the loss of which leaves his survivors the poorer.

There remain for our consideration Gwendolen Erme, Corvick's widow, and Drayton Deane. After Corvick's death the narrator, his curiosity about Vereker's work reviving, finds his only resource to be Gwendolen. If Corvick discovered the secret, he must have related it to his wife. The narrator meditates characteristically: "This was above all what I wanted to know: had *she* seen the idol unveiled? Had there been a private ceremony for a palpitating audience of one? For what else but that ceremony had the nuptials taken place?" Upon being pressed, the widow confesses she has heard the secret, but refuses to expose it: "I heard everything," she replied, "and I mean to keep it to myself."

That Gwendolen really has the secret reveals itself in the increased depth of character she acquires as a result of her bereavement. "Stricken and solitary, highly accomplished and now, in her deep mourning, her maturer grace and her uncomplaining sorrow, incontestably handsome, she presented herself as leading a life of singular dignity and beauty." A year and a half after her husband's death Gwendolen publishes a second novel far superior to her first. Apparently her knowledge of the figure in the carpet, the key to Vereker's work, is evidenced in the greater dimensions of her life and art. She exclaims to the narrator, in dropping her only hint of what the figure is: "It's my *life*!"

Gwendolen marries again; she weds Drayton Deane, a spiritual nonentity very much like the narrator. Her third novel, following her marriage, is inferior to its predecessor. The stream of her life has taken a down turn, and the secret she possessed—given to her by her first husband—seems unable to communicate itself to Deane. The narrator, to his surprise, finds that Deane, after Gwendolen's death, does not have the slightest inkling what the secret is. Both are left forever with an obsession about the secret, the key thrown away.

The idea, accepted by Matthiesson, that James advocates a closer textual criticism, seems to derive less from the story itself than from James' comment on the story for his New York Edition. The comment begins as follows: "I to *this* extent recover the acute impression that may have given birth to 'The Figure in the Carpet,' that no truce, in English-speaking air, had ever seemed to me really struck . . . with our so marked collective mistrust of anything like close or analytic appreciation. . . ." [11] But, in contrast to this statement—written in 1909, thirteen years after the publication of the story—there are James' notebook entries of October 1895, just prior to the writing of the story, in which he speaks of its providing him with a "lovely chance for fine irony on the subject of that fraternity [the critics]." [12] The earlier note seems truer to the story itself; the story ridicules overbusy critics with many touches. The story does not deal centrally with some desired degree of critical analysis, but with the enthusiasm, affection, knowledge, the "sense of life" brought to a work.

As for the secret itself, it is undiscoverable; it reveals the fact that it has been discovered only in the enlarged behavior of its discoverers, not in its being brought to light. "Life" as James' characters live it can be traced in his work; "life," or reality, as an aesthetic concept, as an artistic ingredient, remains a mystique that cannot be formulated.

[11] *The Art of the Novel: Critical Prefaces,* ed. R. P. Blackmur (New York: Charles Scribner's Sons, 1934), p. 227.

[12] *Notebooks,* p. 220.

Art as Problem in "The Figure in the Carpet" and "The Madonna of the Future"

by Charles Feidelson, Jr.

"The art of representation bristles with questions the very terms of which are difficult to apply and to appreciate. . . ."[1] The idea of "art," James's customary key to every problem, was also the most problematic of all his concepts. Though it provided a center for all his thinking, it was always a center of antinomies that multiplied at every turn of his thought. This problematic sense of art is most fully displayed in James's prefaces, which were designed to be a history of his long confrontation with the "veiled face of his Muse."[2] His most concise and general statement in this connection, however, is in a more out-of-the-way place—his curious essay on the subject of personal immortality, "Is There a Life after Death?"[3] Invited to contribute to a symposium of this (for him) unlikely topic, James found his answer, as usual, by appealing to the evidence of his experience as an artist; at the same time, viewing his artistic experience in the light of a kind of ultimate issue he did not often raise explicitly, he was led to spell out the basic problem of his art more philosophically than anywhere else in his works.

The crux of the matter, one gathers here, is the intrinsic ambiguity of the relationship between "consciousness" and "life" in human experience. On the one hand, "consciousness" amounts to no more than

---

[1] Henry James, *The Art of the Novel: Critical Prefaces,* ed. R. P. Blackmur (New York: Charles Scribner's Sons, 1953), p. 3.

[2] Ibid., p. 3.

[3] Henry James, "Is There a Life after Death?" in Henry James, W. D. Howells, et al., *In After Days, Thoughts on the Future Life* (1910), pp. 199–233. Reprinted by F. O. Matthiessen in *The James Family* (New York: Alfred A. Knopf, 1947), 602–14. Subsequent references are to the Matthiessen volume.

a function of "life," and "life" itself, in this perspective, is no more than the natural process of birth, growth, decay, and death. Art, therefore, like all human consciousness, is but an accident of the essentially physical world of nature or of a social world that barely disguises the natural automatism behind it: "our highest flights of personality, our furthest reachings out of the mind, [are] of the very stuff of the abject actual." [4] On the other hand, art is a very special and exemplary kind of human experience; converting "life" into a function of "consciousness," the artist's exercise of imagination amounts to "liv[ing] *in* it." [5] The specifically artistic consciousness *"contain*[*s*] the world" [6] instead of merely being contained by it, and the world it contains, made of quite different stuff from the material life of nature or society, is a universal "being," a metaphysical life which infuses the individual imagination that reaches out and embraces it. The life of imagination, in sum, is an "unlimited vision of being," [7] and it is the unlimited "being" of a visionary mind, rather than a consciousness of vital limits and a vitally limited consciousness. Art, regarded as part of ordinary human experience, finds itself reduced to a relatively trivial manifestation of a natural life in bondage to death, but human consciousness, when regarded as *imaginative* consciousness, turns out to be the avenue to an infinite life, an absolute reality, wherein death is wholly unreal.

These speculations are less interesting in themselves than as an extreme case of James's characteristic logic. As he is careful to say at the end of the essay, he is not propounding a philosophic or religious doctrine; he simply "like[s] to think" [8] in a vein which would issue in idealistic metaphysics if adopted as a "belief." Similarly, he does not reject a naturalistic philosophy any more than he espouses it, for, whatever he may "like to think," he has always been forced to think naturalistically by the very pressure of human experience. Both ways of thinking, in fact, were justified and required by his experience as an artist. In James's artistic practice, it was his quasi-idealism that gave him a place to stand as a writer and gave a direction to the theme of his stories. Transcendent life-in-consciousness was the best rationale that his art could find for itself and the highest value it could hold out to mankind. But it was James's quasi-naturalism that gave him a human voice and a human story to tell. The perennial stimulus for his artistic transcendence, his imaginative embrace of "the thinkable, the possible," was his consciousness-in-life, immersed in the "abject

[4] Ibid., p. 604.
[5] Ibid., p. 609. Italics added.
[6] Ibid., p. 609.
[7] Ibid., p. 610.
[8] Ibid., pp. 613, 614.

actual";[9] and the subject-matter of all his stories—to the end that his art, bemused by "infinite . . . modes of being," should not "lose itself in the ineffable" [10]—was finite actuality, the "bewildered" consciousness of an all-too-natural humanity.[11]

In James's stories about artists, his problematic logic—hinging on the ambiguous relation of "consciousness" to "life" and the ambiguous position of "art" in relation to both—is worked out in many different terms. The basic question posed by James's idealistic and naturalistic readings of the artist's situation reappears in the more concrete dilemmas of his troubled artist-heroes. In the most famous of these stories, "The Figure in the Carpet," the hypothetical "figure" is a problematic meeting-point between artistic creation and imaginative comprehension, the inventive and the critical consciousness, vision and aesthetic formulation. The earthbound critic sits like "a chessplayer bent with a silent scowl, all the lamplit winter, over his board and his moves. . . . On the other side of the table . . . [is] a ghostlier form, the faint figure of an antagonist good-humouredly but a little wearily secure—an antagonist who lean[s] back in his chair with his hands in his pockets and a smile on his fine clear face." [12]

Hugh Vereker, the Master, is a godlike creator, "aloft in his indifference," who dwells in "some safe preserve for sport." [261, 241] He foresees the predestined incomprehension that will greet his books, revels in mystery, and plays a "game" [238] with the world. Yet he is subject to the "unstable moods" of a deity, and he indulges in "one descent from the clouds." [240, 277] Though he is "refined out of existence" like the Joycean and Flaubertian artist, "indifferent, paring his fingernails," he longs to be understood. He invites attention to the meaningful "order, . . . form, . . . texture" [231] of his works. One side of his nature is open: "If my great affair's a secret, that's only because it's a secret in spite of itself—the amazing event has made it one." [232]

The ambiguity of his sublime indifference and his concern, his obscurity and his denial of any such purpose, is visited upon him by the nature of his faculty. For his "little point," his "idea," his "little trick," his "exquisite scheme," as he variously describes it [229–31], both invites and frustrates comprehension. It is neither "something in the style" nor "something in the thought," neither "an element of form" nor "an element of feeling." It is not "a kind of esoteric mes-

[9] Ibid., pp. 604, 605.

[10] Ibid., p. 611.

[11] *The Art of the Novel,* pp. 63–67.

[12] "The Figure in the Carpet," *The Novels and Tales of Henry James,* 25 vols. (New York: Charles Scribner's Sons, 1909), XV, 245. Further page references for this story are given in brackets in the text.

sage . . . some idea about life, some sort of philosophy." [233ff.] In such formulas, the commonplaces of the critical intelligence, he can see only crude questions and pitiful distinctions. His secret, he maintains, is not a "thing" or an "element" of any kind. It does not *refer* to life; it is an "organ of life." Is the heart in your body, he asks, an element of form or an element of feeling? The figure is a vital function of the carpet. "It governs every line, it chooses every word, it dots every i, it places every comma." [233ff.] Therefore its meaning should be public and immediately apprehensible; and yet it baffles the public mind by subtly altering the status of "life," putting itself above the limited and limiting categories in which life ordinarily comes to consciousness.

On their different plane, the narrator and his intensely "literary" friends are no less governed by a paradoxical principle beyond their control. For them, "literature was a game of skill, and skill meant courage, and courage meant honour, and honour meant passion, meant life. The stake on the table was of a special substance and . . . [their] roulette the revolving mind, but . . . [they] sat around the green board as intently as the grim gamblers at Monte Carlo." [250] It is the mission of these dedicated spirits to break the bank, to convert the special substance of art into the standard currency of the revolving mind. But the devotee is fated to "bound off on false scents . . . clap his hands over new lights and see them blown out by the wind of the turned page." [244] He dwells in the very "temples of chance," [250] and his skill is incommensurable with the absolute he courts.

This predicament gives rise to the farcical situation at the feet of the Master: the hot little egos in quest of "buried treasure." [235] If Vereker retreats into his heaven of silence, these homunculi descend from their high pretensions to the noisy earth. The worst offender is the narrator, who meets Vereker's confidence with "cheap journalese," [233] later lapses into sceptical jeering, and for the most part tells the story in a cheeky, rancorous tone. His incorrigibly mundane mind insists that the "immense" secret can "be got into a letter" unless "it's immense bosh." [252] The penalty of his oversimplification is the obsession that comes to ride him: expecting the revelation in capsule, he remains a "victim of unappeased desire." [277] Yet even the redoubtable Corvick and the more redoubtable Gwendolen Erme, who claim to have grasped the secret in terms acceptable to Vereker himself, convey no impression of disinterested illumination. Whatever Corvick told the novelist—and one is suspicious of the whole transaction—it began to be vulgarized as soon as he and it reentered the world of telegrams, intellectual love-affairs, projected articles, and literary vanity. Corvick's death is accidental, but surely saves him from the discovery that his article will never be written; and the magic formula has certainly evaporated in the hands of Gwendolen, who broods over it like a miser.

The aspirations of both Vereker and his disciples depend on the relation of imaginative consciousness to "life." Just as the gist of the Master's complaint is that "nobody has ever mentioned . . . the organ of life" in his work [234], his followers feel that the pursuit of "literature" is nothing less than the pursuit of "life"; for them, the skill of the one merges with the courage, honour, passion of the other. Gwendolen clasps the secret to her bosom with the cry, "It's my *life*!" [266] For Corvick, the best of the lot, "a question of art" or of "letters" or of "life" is "all one thing." [242] If he never falls into the narrator's wholly reductive attitude, and if there is reason to think that he will "come out somewhere," [244] it is because he conceives the figure as a vital apprehension—he has "caught whiffs and hints of he didn't know what, faint wandering notes of hidden music." [244] We are given to understand that his revelation springs upon him "like a tigress out of the jungle . . . in the *secousse* of a new and intense experience." [251 ff.] Though his meeting of minds with Vereker takes place offstage and reaches us only in a debased account, it symbolizes complete realization of a theoretical possibility which is assumed throughout the story: a common imaginative life in which the Master's transcendent life-as-consciousness and the critic's consciousness, immanent in life, would merge into one.

But the fact that the encounter remains a mere postulate is thoroughly in keeping with the concept it symbolizes. "Angel, write," is Gwendolen's telegram [253]; yet we never hear Corvick's evangel because imaginative life is experienced only as the putative harmony of two distinct keys or inflections, quasi-divine and quasi-human. It takes on different colorations as it is pursued on a transcendent or an immanent level. The kind associated with Vereker is generalized, monistic, a priori, absolutist. In a pure state, it would be an activity without obstacles, a process without struggle—"an intenser experience," as James once said, ". . . a sublime security like that enjoyed on the flowery plains of heaven, where we may conceive ourselves proceeding in ecstasy from one prodigious phase and form of it to another." [13] The opposite of this divine process is the world of Vereker's coterie, who are committed to the conditional, the pluralistic, the historical, the relative. They are *in* a process they endlessly seek to understand, moving from point to point (in another Jamesian phrase) through "lapses and compromises, simplifications and surrenders." [14] They evince the work of all workings, a secular experience of insecurity and operative will.

[13] *The Art of the Novel*, p. 32.
[14] Ibid., p. 126.

Primarily, this is not a cautionary tale, as James's comments in his preface tend to suggest, but the ironic legend of an aspiration that contains its own fatality. The much earlier story of Theobald, the romantic painter of "The Madonna of the Future," displays the same general constellation of terms and makes the problematic theme even more explicit. In both cases, the doom consists in the breakdown of imaginative life—or whatever we want to call that elusive meeting-point—into opposite versions; and beyond this it consists in the grotesque self-parody of the transcendent and the immanent that results from their disjunction. In "The Figure in the Carpet," Vereker is let off lightly, although there is more than a suggestion of defeat in his proud withdrawal into his citadel. The secularists are the losers. In "The Madonna of the Future," the case is put the other way: Theobald is doomed. But the large-scale problem is the same: "I'm the half of a genius!" says Theobald. "Where in the wide world is my other half? Lodged perhaps in the vulgar soul, the cunning ready fingers of some dull copyist or some trivial artisan who turns out by the dozen his easy prodigies of touch!" [15]

This artisan actually appears in the story. He is a sculptor, clever and impudent, who has invented "a peculiar plastic compound" and specializes in statuettes of cats and monkeys "in . . . preposterously sentimental conjunction." [481, 482] Theobald scarcely does justice to him or to his half of the world. The sculptor's sole claim to esteem is not, as Theobald supposes, the mere fact that "he at least does something" while Theobald "can't act, . . . can't do nor dare." [486, 487] He is "a man of imagination," as he intimates, and of an imagination harnessed to "human life." [482, 483] With conscious irony he propounds his own worldly version of that ambiguous formula. Let the romantic aspire to "complete artistic vision"; the sculptor is not without his secular correlative, for his own potential "combinations" are "really infinite." [452, 483] Let Theobald seek to enshrine life in a Madonna, a "perfect eternal type" abstracted from "the struggle for existence"; this denizen of the struggle, by means of a "little stroke of chemical ingenuity," can also offer types "firm as alabaster . . . durable as bronze—*aere perennius,* signore—and . . . more amusing!" [468, 482ff.] It is true (and he concedes) that his statuettes are also "light as cork," [481] but here we must turn to "Madonna Serafina," the massive Italian woman who is his mistress and Theobald's model. Since the moment long ago when Theobald saw her as the Madonna reincarnate, as "she might have stepped out of the stable of Bethle-

[15] "The Madonna of the Future," *The Novels and Tales of Henry James* (New York: Charles Scribner's Sons, 1908), XIII, 487. Further page references for this story are given in brackets in the text.

hem," [470] sheer duration may have given a weight of meaning to Theobald's vision of her, but time has given her the weight of experience that the sculptor embraces.

Repellent as they seem to the high-minded narrator, the values of the monkey and the cat, the sculptor and his mistress, point toward something positive. As the narrator himself has already discovered, cognate principles are required in order to account for the very masterpieces that Theobald adores. For all the distance between the sculptor and Raphael, one must suppose that "the Raphaelesque touch, . . . as calculating and commercial as any other," made the Madonna of the Chair out of the transient life of "some pretty young woman." [449, 451] The type of the Virgin, however Theobald may protest that it is "one of the eternal needs of man's heart," is demonstrably one of the passing products of human history, which created "a demand for the Blessed Virgin" and now has other demands. [451] This is not a lapse into cynicism; the narrator perceives that art is a positive acceptance of such conditions. "The vulgar effort and hazard of production" [474] is defined as heroic enterprise in the masterpieces that arise from it. At the beginning of the story, a street that looks "as if it bored into the heart of Florence" leads him to two statues that are "images" of secular life and imagination. [438] The first, Michelangelo's David, expresses human strength and alertness in the face of the perilous accidents of existence. The young man is glad to look away from that "heroic sinister strength," but he does so in order to contemplate Cellini's Perseus, the emblem of a less sublime art which is no less an exercise of heroic virtue. Perseus signifies the artistic norm of which "monkeys and cats" are the aberrant extreme: "a figure supremely shapely and graceful, markedly gentle almost," he holds out "with his light nervous arm the snaky head of the slaughtered Gorgon." [438ff.]

In the collapse of his hopes, Theobald momentarily glimpses the artist as Perseus. He recognizes that even Michelangelo made the statue of Lorenzo in something like the spirit of the Medici: "He did his best at a venture, and his venture's immortal." [486] Theobald proclaims that he himself should have espoused that ethos, even in its lowest form of the "vulgar and clever and reckless." [487] But in fact he is so constituted that he cannot long conceive of the secular mode except in its lowest form; for him, "the hand, the will" have no intrinsic worth but are at best instrumental to "the ideal." [486, 449] And he has reason; after all, there must be a basic shift of emphasis somewhere in the chain of relation between Serafina's lover and Michelangelo. Primarily, Theobald would say, the artist is "a seer" who exemplifies the virtues of "vision" rather than "labour." [449, 486, 444] The Madonna, his "model . . . and muse," is the emblem of the power of transcendence that creates her—that miraculously "intensifies" the "rich realities of nature" so as to extract her "spotless image" out of "the foul vapours of life." [449, 450] She is, and she sanctions, an experience so abstract that it is "form made perfect," and so comprehensive that "the man who paints it has painted everything." [449, 452]

What Theobald does not foresee, but suffers, is the paradoxical consequence of his brand of "idealism." [450] He can truly say that in his own fashion he is "at work" and that his motto is "Invent, create, achieve." [442, 443] But his quest for the form of all forms entails that he shall be forever at work, beset by "phantasmal pictures" until "life burn[s] out in delirium"; [489] or that he shall achieve a work ("the completion of the Madonna" [474]) which is devoid of life: the empty canvas that stands in his room. Both aspects of his fate are what the narrator perceives in the object on the easel: the Madonna of an illusory future, "cracked and discoloured by time," and "the mere dead blank" of a transcendent form. [485]

Near the conclusion of the story, at Theobald's funeral, the narrator has a significant exchange with Mrs. Coventry, one of Theobald's chief detractors. He tells her that he has seen the long-awaited Madonna and that it belongs to him "by bequest." [489] This lady, "a social high-priestess of the arts" who recalls Gwendolyn Erme, "always wore on her bosom a huge, if reduced, copy of the Madonna della Seggiola." [458] In Theobald's words, she "profanes sacred things," and the narrator declares that he will not show her the painting because she "wouldn't understand." [462, 490] No more could Theobald, the "saint," understand "profane experience." [456] What the narrator has inherited is the problem embodied in the empty canvas and the correlative problem embodied in a refrain that rings in his ears—"Cats and monkeys, monkeys and cats—all human life is there!" [482, 492] The only intermediary is another phrase, "He did his best at a venture." [486, 490] But how, existing by venture, did Michelangelo avoid "cats and monkeys"? And how, avoiding cats and monkeys, did he escape "Theobald's transcendent illusions and deplorable failure"? [492]

Caught in this dilemma, "sad and vexed and bitter," [490] the narrator beholds in a new and tragic light the masterpieces of the galleries, the indubitable fact of successful art. His final mood was anticipated early in the story, when the statue of Lorenzo seemed to "sit like some awful Genius of Doubt and brood behind his eternal mask upon the mysteries of life." [455] Later the mysterious verged toward the tyrannous and the sinister. In his last visit with Theobald to the galleries, the pictures "glowed, to my stricken sight, with an insolent renewal of strength and lustre. . . . The celestial candour even of the Madonna of the Chair . . . broke into the strange smile of the women of Leonardo." [487] Finally, returning to the Medici chapel, he senses "the sadness of its immortal treasures," and "the ruins of triumphant Rome," where he seeks escape, betoken a fatal flaw at the heart of all imaginative triumph. [490, 492]

It is not merely the menace of time that makes for this "sadness" of art, any more than it is mere survival in time that accounts for the "insolence" of the Florentine masterpieces. It is the element of the fortuitous in the highest imaginative achievement that art seems to be sadly confessing, and the element of the absolute in sheer fabrication that it seems to be insolently flaunting. In either case, the "Genius of Doubt" appropriately presides over the scene of the story, an art-world that mainly bespeaks the inner contradictions of artistry, the "veiled face of . . . [the] Muse." [16] In "The Figure in the Carpet"—though the polarities there are less starkly presented and the final tone is much less grim—the thrust of James's problematic logic goes even further. For the "figure," unlike the statues of David and Perseus and Lorenzo in "The Madonna of the Future," is a mere potentiality, and imaginative essence that actually exists only in two mutually exclusive ways. If the earlier tale casts doubt on the genesis of art, the later brings imaginative reality itself into question.

It is true that such stories are high abstractions, and perhaps they arrive at a thematic impasse in a too obviously calculated way. Though they may be contrived, however, they are not merely willful or fantastic. They lead us back to the peculiar temper of the mind that conjured them up, the mind of an artist who flourished on dubiety, made himself artistically at home amid questions that endlessly "bristle[d]" within every exercise of his faculty. In James's experience, the "art of representation" forever multiplied, never solved, the problems latent in itself, yet his awareness of unresolved problems forever enlarged his sense of the purport of what he was doing when he engaged in imaginative work: "whatever makes it arduous . . . causes the practice of it . . . to spread round us in a widening, not in a narrowing circle." [17] Translated into the subject-matter of fiction, James's experience of the problematical in art yielded the artist-fable; this kind of ironic legend, half-farcical and half-tragic, was his most immediate interpretation of the circles of significance that seemed to inhere in the dubious practice of fiction. Beyond it were other circles, rendered in the fictional world of his greater stories and his novels, where the "Genius of Doubt" became the underlying principle, at once the fate and the glory, of an imaginative mankind.

16 *The Art of the Novel,* p. 3.

17 Ibid., p. 3.

Edmund Wilson and *The Turn of the Screw*

by M. Slaughter

For thirty-six years after James published his instantaneously popular *The Turn of the Screw,* the tale was generally read as a marvelously contrived, but pure and simple, ghost-story. There were dissenters from this proposition—principally Edna Kenton, who in 1924 suggested that the center of the reader's attention should be placed not on the haunted children, but on the governess who is "pathetically trying to harmonize her own disharmonies by creating discords outside herself" (*The Arts,* VI, November, 1924, 254). The tale, not at all a mere fairy-tale, was a sophisticated amusette carefully designed to trick the unwary reader. When Edmund Wilson in the spring of 1934 published "The Ambiguity of Henry James" in *Hound & Horn,* VII (April–May, 1934, 385–406), this minority view received a clear and forthright annunciation.

I

Wilson found a base in Miss Kenton's suggestion of the governess's neuroticism. The governess is indeed disturbed, but according to Wilson's Freudian point of view, the nature of her trouble is explicitly sexual. She is one of James's familiar types—"the frustrated Anglo-Saxon spinster" (*Hound & Horn,* VII, April–May, 1934, 391)—and in the role of narrator actually rationalizes, justifies, and screens her personal inadequacy. For Wilson, then, the tale holds "another mystery beneath the ostensible one" (VII, 385). Her account of the ghosts is not distorted; the ghosts simply do not exist. Wilson believed that "the young governess who tells the story is a neurotic case of sex repression, and the ghosts are not real ghosts at all but merely the governess's hallucinations" (VII, 385). The tale has "a false hypothesis

"Edmund Wilson and The Turn of the Screw," *by M. Slaughter. From Henry James,* The Turn of the Screw, *Norton Critical Edition, ed. Robert Kimbrough, pp. 211–14.*

which the narrator is putting forward and a reality which we are supposed to divine" (VII, 395).

Wilson justified this psychological interpretation by saying that "there is never any evidence that anybody but the governess sees the ghosts" (VII, 387). Miles and Flora never really admit their existence. In the final scene, it is not implausible to attribute Miles's reaction to confusion and fright. Mrs. Grose seemingly comes over to the governess's side, but it is impossible to determine whether she believes in the ghosts or is merely placating her superior. The hallucination theory, however, might falter over one question: if the ghosts are products of her own mind, how can she, independently and accurately, without any previous knowledge of him, describe the apparition as Quint? For the time being, Wilson rested with a rather inscrutable answer: evidently Quint and the master strongly resembled one another and the governess had merely confused the two (VII, 388).

As Wilson saw it, the governess's self-conceived apparitions were projections resulting from sexual desire and frustration. After she fell in love with her handsome employer, she nursed her feelings with fantasies and much of her later behavior is motivated by her desire to impress him. We are supposed to feel that there is something obsessive about her repeated attempts to prove herself to a man she has met only once and may never see again. Her latent sexual frustrations are further revealed in her strikingly possessive and intimate attitude toward little Miles. The final clue is given in several well-placed, significant Freudian symbols: Quint on the tower; Miss Jessel at the lake; Flora's toy boat, which she makes by pushing a stick into a small flat piece of wood (VII, 387).

According to Wilson, then, James had intentionally created the governess as an ambiguous, neurotic character. Behind the façade of the ghost-story was the real tale, "a study in morbid psychology" (VII, 390): the governess was intentionally created as an ambiguous, neurotic character. In its vexing blend of the psychological and supernatural, the tale belongs to a group of fairy-tales "whose symbols exert a peculiar power by reason of the fact that they have behind them, whether or not the authors are aware of it, a profound grasp of subconscious processes" (VII, 390–91).

II

The extremity of Wilson's position and his avowed Freudian bias stimulated a literary controversy which, over the years, has become itself almost as compelling as the tale. Forced by critical pressure to reconsider his interpretation, Wilson followed up the original essay with a series of revisions and retractions, so that almost as much attention has been devoted to Wilson as to James. The criticism has become almost as interesting as the work, the critic almost as central as the author.

When Wilson revised his essay four years later for inclusion in *The Triple Thinkers* (Harcourt, Brace and Co.: New York, 1938), he seems to have had some doubts about his original interpretation. In the revision, not "everything" but "almost everything" (p. 130) in the tale could be read in either of two senses. In the late forties, critical pressure continued to bear down. A. J. A. Waldock, in "Mr. Edmund Wilson and *The Turn of the Screw*," questioned the identification of Quint: "How did the governess succeed in projecting on vacancy, out of her own self-conscious mind, a perfectly precise, point-by-point image of a man, then dead, whom she had never seen in her life and never heard of? What psychology, normal or abnormal, will explain that? And what is the right word for such a vision but 'ghost'?" (*Modern Language Notes,* LXII, May, 1947, 333–34). Robert B. Heilman, among others, went outside the text to James's Preface to Volume XII of the New York Edition for evidence to refute Wilson ("The Freudian Reading of *The Turn of the Screw*," *MLN,* LXII, November, 1947, 433–45). And, in 1947, when the *Notebooks* were first published, further evidence was offered which seemed to indicate that James did indeed intend to write a bona fide ghost-story.

III

As an apparent result of this assault, Wilson in the second and expanded edition of *Triple Thinkers* (Oxford University Press: New York, 1948) restated his thesis, conceding that he had "forced a point" (p. 123) in his explanation of the identification of Quint, and backing away from his original contention that James had consciously intended the governess's tale to be ambiguous. Wilson now observed that the story was written at a time when the author's "faith in himself had been somewhat shaken" (p. 123): his self-doubts were unintentionally and unconsciously incorporated into the character of the governess. James's personal and authorial blind spot was sex, and his inability to confront, perhaps even to understand, sexual feelings, was transformed into the ambiguity of the governess. Wilson concluded that "in *The Turn of the Screw,* not merely is the governess self-deceived, but that James is self-deceived about her" (p. 125).

IV

By 1959, however, relying mainly on an article by John Silver, "A Note on the Freudian Reading of 'The Turn of the Screw'," Wilson was partially able to resolve his ambiguity about James's ambiguity; Silver extricated Wilson from his difficulties over the governess's identification of Quint by arguing that she had learned of his appearance from the neighboring villagers (*American Literature,* XXIX, May, 1957, 207–11). Then, focussing once more on the author's conscious use and manipulation of the first-person narrator in this tale and the other stories with which it is bound in Volume XII of the New York Edition, Wilson, in a short note appended to a reprint of the 1948 version of his essay, was again "convinced that James knew exactly what he was doing and that he intended the governess to be suffering from delusions." Her mind is "warped," the story she tells is "untrue" (*A Casebook on Henry James's "The Turn of the Screw,"* Thomas Y. Crowell Co.: New York, 1960, p. 153). He did not mention, this time, the possible sexual origin of the governess's distortion.

Wilson's original thesis no longer startles, but it and the controversy which followed it so changed the winds of Jamesian criticism that many critics today remain divided into two camps: that which sees a ghost-story and that which sees a psychological study. In a recent book, Krishna B. Vaid has pronounced the governess absolutely straightforward and reliable (*Technique in the Tales of Henry James,* Harvard University Press: Cambridge, Mass., 1964). But more recently, Thomas M. Cranfill and Robert L. Clark, Jr. have written a book to prove the opposite (*An Anatomy of The Turn of the Screw,* University of Texas Press: Austin, 1965).

A Pre-Freudian Reading of *The Turn of the Screw*

by Harold C. Goddard

Prefatory Note by Leon Edel: The following essay on Henry James's *The Turn of the Screw* was discovered among the posthumous papers of the late Harold C. Goddard, professor of English and former head of the department at Swarthmore College. According to Professor Goddard's daughter, Eleanor Goddard Worthen, he read this essay to generations of students, but made no attempt to have it published. It was written, she says, "about 1920 or before," and this is evident from the critics he mentions, no one later than William Lyon Phelps. The manuscript was communicated by her to Edmund Wilson, whose 1934 essay on "The Ambiguity of Henry James" first propounded the hallucination theory of *The Turn of the Screw* with a bow in the direction of an earlier essay by the late Edna Kenton. Mr. Wilson, in turn, sent the Goddard paper to me and we both agreed that even at this late date, when the ink flows so freely around the Jamesian ghostly tale, it should be made available to scholars and critics.

To Professor Goddard must now go the credit of being the first to expound, if not to publish, a hallucination theory of the story. Indeed he went much farther than Mr. Wilson was to go after him—and without the aid of Sigmund Freud. Goddard's essay is a singularly valuable example of textual study. He relied wholly on what James had written, and he gave the tale that attentive reading which the novelist invited when he called his work a "trap for the unwary." Professor Goddard does not seem to have been aware, when he read the tale, that there was a "trap" in it. He is the only reader of *The Turn of the Screw* I have found who not only sought to understand the psychology of the governess but examined the heroine from the viewpoint of the children entrusted to her. No other critic has paid attention to

---

the governess' account of the wild look in her own eyes, the terror in her face. Above all, however, we must be grateful to Professor Goddard's scrupulous analysis of the "identification" scene—the scene in which Mrs. Grose is led, step by step, to pronounce the name of Peter Quint. Even the most confirmed hallucinationists have never done sufficient justice to the ambiguity of this scene.

Before the discovery of this essay, Edna Kenton's "Henry James to the Ruminant Reader" published in *The Arts* in November, 1924, stood as the first to attract attention to the importance of the point of view in the tale: the fact that the story is told entirely through the governess' eyes. Miss Kenton did not suggest in her published essay the idea attributed to her by Edmund Wilson that the governess represented a "neurotic case of sex-repression." This idea was wholly Mr. Wilson's, and earlier seems to have been Ezra Pound's, who called the tale "a Freudian affair." Miss Kenton's article is patently innocent of any such theory, and those critics who have spoken of the "Kenton-Wilson" theory of *The Turn of the Screw* quite obviously had read only Wilson, not Kenton.

With the studies of Goddard, Kenton and Wilson before us, I would suggest that three points are now clearly established: (1) that Henry James wrote a ghost story, a psychological thriller, intended to arouse a maximum of horror in the minds of his readers; (2) that a critical reading of the story to see how James achieved his horror reveals that he maneuvered the reader into the position of believing the governess' story even though her account contains serious contradictions and a purely speculative theory of her own as to the nature and purpose of the apparitions, which she alone sees; (3) that anyone wishing to treat the governess as a psychological "case" is offered sufficient data to permit the diagnosis that she is mentally disturbed. It is indeed valid to speculate that James, in speaking of a "trap," was alluding not only to the question of the governess' credibility as a witness, but to her actual madness.

There is one particular aspect of Professor Goddard's paper which we must not neglect. I refer to the fact that he was able to relate the story to his own memory of a governess he had when he was a boy. I think this important because it represents the use of the reader's personal experience for which James made so large an allowance—as he confided to his doctor, Sir James Mackenzie, who questioned him about the story, and also as he explained in his preface: that is James's refusal to specify the "horrors" so that the reader might fill them in for himself. Goddard's experience happened to be particularly close to the very elements in the story. There was thus a happy conjunction of personal fact with his "factual" reading. . . .

A good many years ago I came upon *The Turn of the Screw* for the first time. I supposed I already knew what it was to be gripped by a powerful tale. But before I had read twenty pages I realized I had never encountered anything of this sort before. From the first, one of the things that chiefly struck me about James's tale was the way in which it united the thrills one is entitled to expect from a ghost story with the quality of being entirely credible, even by daylight. True, it evoked plenty of mystery, propounded plenty of enigmas, along the way. But the main idea of the thing was perfectly plain. So at any rate I thought. For it never occurred to me that there could be two opinions about that. What was my surprise, then, on taking it up with a group of students, to discover that not one of them interpreted it as I did. My faith in what seemed to me the obvious way of taking the story would have been shaken, had I not, on explaining it, found the majority of my fellow readers ready to prefer it to their own. And this experience was repeated with later groups. Yet, even after several years, it had not occurred to me that what seemed the natural interpretation of the narrative was not the generally accepted one among critics, however little it might be among students. And then one day I ran on a comment of Mr. Chesterton's on the story. He took it precisely as my students had. I began watching out in my reading for allusions to the story. I looked up several references to it. They all agreed. Evidently my view was utterly heretical. Naturally I asked myself more sharply than ever why I should take the tale as a matter of course in a way that did not seem to occur to other readers. Was it perversity on my part, or profundity? And then one day it dawned over me that perhaps it was neither. Perhaps it was the result rather of a remarkable parallelism between a strange passage in my own early experience (of which I will tell at the proper time) and what I conceived to be the situation in *The Turn of the Screw*. However that may be, at every rereading of the story I found myself adhering more firmly than ever to my original idea, and I continued to find that it met with hospitable reception among others. Not that there were no skeptics. Or now and then a strenuous objector.

It was not until long afterward that I happened to read James's own comment on *The Turn of the Screw* in the introduction to the collected edition of his works. A man with an hypothesis runs the risk of finding confirmation for it everywhere. Still, I set down for what it is worth the fact that in this introduction I thought I detected a very clear, but very covert, corroboration of the interpretation I favored, and later still, I got a similar impression, on the publication of James's letters, from passages referring to the story.

I

From the point of view of early critics of the tale [Chesterton, Rebecca West, Carl Van Doren, Stuart P. Sherman, William Lyon Phelps, and others], the story may be summarized, in bare outline, as follows:

An English gentleman, by the death of his brother in India, becomes guardian of a small niece and nephew whom he places in charge of a governess at his country home, Bly. On his departure from Bly, he leaves behind him his valet, a certain Peter Quint, with whom the governess, Miss Jessel, soon grows intimate. The valet is thus thrown in close contact with the children, with the boy in particular, who goes about with him as if he were his tutor. Quint and Miss Jessel are a depraved pair and the children do not escape exposure to their evil. As to the details of the contamination they suffer the author leaves us mercifully in the dark. But it is easy enough to guess its general nature. A point at any rate that is certain is the character of the language that the children pick up from their two protectors: language the use of which, later, was the cause of the boy's mysterious expulsion from school. Prior to this, however, Peter Quint, while drunk, slips on the ice and is killed, and Miss Jessel, whose reason for leaving Bly is broadly hinted, goes away—to die.

The world seems well rid of such a pair. But it turns out otherwise. For it is precisely at this point that the full horror of the situation develops and the infernal character of the tale emerges. Such, it transpires, was the passion of Quint and Miss Jessel to possess the souls of the innocent children that they return to their old haunts *after death,* appearing to their helpless victims and infecting them still further with their evil. Meanwhile, however, a new governess has been procured, who, fortunately for the children, is herself susceptible to visitation from the world beyond, and who, accordingly, does not long remain in the dark as to what is going on. Moved by a love for her little charges and a pity for them as deep as were the opposite emotions of their former companions, she attempts to throw herself as a screen between them and the discarnate fiends who pursue them, hoping that by accepting, as it were, the first shock of the impact she may shield and ultimately save the innocent children. In her protracted and lonely struggle with the agents of evil, she succeeds, but at a fearful price. The children are indeed dispossessed. But the little girl is driven in the proces into a delirium which threatens the impairment of her intellect, while the boy expires at the very moment when he is snatched back from the brink of the abyss down which he is slipping.

So taken, the story is susceptible equally of two interpretations. It may be conceived, literally, as an embodiment of the author's belief in survival after death and in the power of spirits, in this case of evil spirits, to visit the living upon earth. Or, if one prefers, it may be taken as an allegory, in manner not unlike *Dr. Jekyll and Mr. Hyde:* the concrete representation of the truth that the evil that men do lives after them, infecting life long after they themselves are gone. Either way, except for the heroism of the second governess, the story is one of almost unmitigated horror. One can understand Mr. Chesterton's doubt as to whether the thing ought ever to have been published.

II

It is possible, however, to question the fidelity of either of these versions to the facts of the story and to ask whether another interpretation is not possible which will redeem the narrative from the charge of ugliness and render even its horror subordinate to its beauty.

Consider the second governess for a moment and the situation in which she finds herself. She is a young woman, only twenty, the daughter of a country parson, who, from his daughter's one allusion to him in her story, is of a psychically unbalanced nature; he may, indeed, even have been insane. We are given a number of oblique glimpses into the young woman's home and early environment. They all point to its stifling narrowness. From the confinement of her provincial home this young and inexperienced woman comes up to London to answer an advertisement for a governess. That in itself constitutes a sufficient crisis in the life of one who, after one glimpse, we do not need to be told is an excessively nervous and emotional person. But to add to the intensity of the situation the young woman falls instantly and passionately in love with the man who has inserted the advertisement. She scarcely admits it even to herself, for in her heart she knows that her love is hopeless, the object of her affection being one socially out of her sphere, a gentleman who can never regard her as anything other than a governess. But even this is not all. In her overwrought condition, the unexplained death of the former governess, her predecessor, was enough to suggest some mysterious danger connected with the position offered, especially in view of the master's strange stipulation: that the incumbent should assume *all* responsibility, even to the point of cutting off all communication with him—never writing, never reporting. Something extraordinary, she was convinced, lurked in the background. She would never have accepted the place if it had not been for her newborn passion: she could not bring herself to disappoint him when he seemed to beg compliance of her as a favor—to say nothing of severing her only link with the man who had so powerfully attracted her.

So she goes down to Bly, this slip of a girl, and finds herself no longer a poor parson's daughter but, quite literally, the head of a considerable country establishment. As if to impart the last ingredient to the witch's broth of her emotions, she is carried away almost to the point of ecstasy by the beauty of the two children, Miles and Flora, who have been confided to her care. All this could supply the material for a nervous breakdown in a girl of no worldly experience and of unstable psychical background. At any rate she instantly becomes the victim of insomnia. The very first night she fancies that she hears a light footstep outside her door and in the far distance the cry of a child. And more serious symptoms soon appear.

But before considering these, think what would be bound to happen even to a more normal mentality in such a situation. When a young person, especially a young woman, falls in love and circumstances forbid the normal growth and confession of the passion, the emotion, dammed up, overflows in a psychical experience, a daydream, or internal drama which the mind creates in lieu of the thwarted realization in the objective world. In romantic natures this takes the form of imagined deeds of extraordinary heroism or self-sacrifice done in behalf of the beloved object. The governess' is precisely such a nature and the fact that she knows her love is futile intensifies the tendency. Her whole being tingles with the craving to perform some act of unexampled courage. To carry out her duties as governess is not enough. They are too humdrum. If only the house would take fire by night, and both the children be in peril! Or if one of them would fall into the water! But no such crudely melodramatic opportunities occur. What does occur is something far more indefinite, far more provocative to the imaginative than to the active faculties: the boy, Miles, is dismissed from school for no assigned or assignable reason. Once more, the hint of something evil and extraordinary behind the scenes! It is just the touch of objectivity needed to set off the subconsciousness of the governess into an orgy of myth-making. Another woman of a more practical and common sense turn would have made inquiries, would have followed the thing up, would have been insistent. But it is precisely complication and not explanation that this woman wants—though of course she does not know it. The vague feeling of fear with which the place is invested for her is fertile soil for imaginative invention and an inadvertent hint about Peter Quint dropped by the housekeeper, Mrs. Grose, is just the seed that that soil requires. There is no more significant bit of dialogue in the story. Yet the reader, unless he is alert, is likely to pass it by unmarked. The governess and the housekeeper are exchanging confidences. The former asks:

"What was the lady who was here before?"

"The last governess? She was also young and pretty—almost as young and almost as pretty, Miss, even as you."

"Ah then I hope her youth and her beauty helped her!" I recollect throwing off. "He seems to like us young and pretty!"

"Oh he *did*," Mrs. Grose assented: "it was the way he liked everyone!" She had no sooner spoken indeed than she caught herself up. "I mean that's *his* way—the master's."

I was struck. "But of whom did you speak first?"

She looked blank, but she coloured. "Why, of *him*."

"Of the master?"

"Of who else?"

There was so obviously no one else that the next moment I had lost my impression of her having accidentally said more than she meant.

The consciousness of the governess may have lost its impression, but we do not need to be students of psychology to know that that inveterate playwright and stage manager, the subconscious, would never permit so valuable a hint to go unutilized.

Mrs. Grose, as her coloring shows and as the governess discerns, is thinking of some one other than the master. Of what man would she naturally think, on the mention of Miss Jessel, if not of Miss Jessel's running mate and partner in evil, Peter Quint? It is a momentary slip, but it is none the less fatal. It supplies the one character missing in the heroic drama that the governess' repressed desire is bent on staging: namely, the villain. The hero of that drama is behind the scenes: the master in Harley Street. The heroine, of course, is the governess herself. The villain, as we said, is this unknown man who "liked them young and pretty." The first complication in the plot is the mysterious dismissal of the boy from school, suggestive of some dim power of evil shadowing the child. The plot itself remains to be worked out, but it will inevitably turn on some act of heroism or self-sacrifice—both by preference—on the part of the heroine for the benefit of the hero and to the discomfiture of the villain. It is a foregone conclusion, too, that the villain will be in some way connected with the boy's predicament at school. (That he really was is a coincidence.) All this is not conjecture. It is elemental human psychology.

Such is the material and plan upon which the dreaming consciousness of the governess sets to work. But how dream when one is the victim of insomnia? Daydream, then? But ordinary daydreams are not enough for the passionate nature of the governess. So she proceeds to act her drama out, quite after the fashion of a highly imaginative child at play. And the first scene of her dramatic creation is compressed into the few moments when she sees the stranger on the tower of Bly by twilight.

Whence does that apparition come? *Out of the governess's unconfessed love and unformulated fear.* It is clearly her love that first evokes him, for, as she tells us, she was thinking, as she strolled about the grounds that afternoon, how charming it would be suddenly to meet "some one," to have "some one" appear at the turn of a path and stand before her and smile and approve, when suddenly, with the face she longed to see still vividly present to her mind, she stopped short. "What arrested me on the spot," she says, "—and with a shock much greater than any vision had allowed for—was the sense that my imagination had, in a flash, turned real. He did stand there!—but high up, beyond the lawn and at the very top of the tower. . . ." Instantly, however, she perceives her mistake. It is not he. In her heart she knows it cannot be. But if her love is too good to be true, her fears, unfortunately, are only too true. And forthwith those fears seize and transform this creation of her imagination. "It produced in me," the governess declares, "this figure, in the clear twilight, I remember, two distinct gasps of emotion, which were, sharply, the shock of my first and that of my second surprise. My second was a violent perception of the mistake of my first: the man who met my eyes was not the person I had precipitately supposed. There came to me thus a bewilderment of vision of which, after these years, there is no living view that I can hope to give." What has happened? The hint that the housekeeper dropped of an unnamed man in the neighborhood has done its work. Around that hint the imagination of the governess precipitates the specter who is to dominate the rest of the tale. And because he is an object of dread he is no sooner evoked than he becomes the raw material of heroism. It only remains to link him with the children and the "play" will be under way with a rush.

This linking takes place on the Sunday afternoon when the governess, just as she is about to go out to church, becomes suddently aware of a man gazing in at the dining room window. Instantly there comes over her, as she puts it, the "shock of a certitude that it was not for me he had come. He had come for some one else." "The flash of this knowledge," she continues, "—for it was knowledge in the midst of dread—produced in me the most extraordinary effect, starting, as I stood there, a sudden vibration of duty and courage." The governess feels her sudden vibration of duty and courage as the effect of the apparition, but it would be closer to the truth to call it its cause. Why has the stranger come for the children rather than for her? Because she must not merely be brave; she must be brave for someone's sake. The hero must be brought into the drama. She must save the beings whom he has commissioned her to protect. And that she may have the opportunity to save them they must be menaced: they must have enemies. That is the creative logic of her hallucination.

"Hallucination!" a dozen objectors will cry, unable to hold in any longer. "Why! the very word shows that you have missed the whole point of the story. The creature at the window is no hallucination. It is he himself, Peter Quint, returned from the dead. If not, how was Mrs. Grose able to recognize him—and later Miss Jessel—from the governess's description?"

The objection seems well taken. The point, indeed, is a capital one with the governess herself, who clings to it as unshakable proof that she is not mad; for Mrs. Grose, it appears, though she seems to accept her companion's account of her strange experiences, has moments of backsliding, of toying with the hypothesis that the ghosts are mere creatures of the governess' fancy. Whereupon, says the latter, "I had only to ask her how, if I had 'made it up,' I came to be able to give, of each of the persons appearing to me, a picture disclosing, to the last detail, their special marks—a portrait on the exhibition of which she had instantly recognized and named them." This retort floors Mrs. Grose completely, and she wishes "to sink the whole subject."

But Mrs. Grose is a trustful soul, too easily floored perhaps. If we will look into the matter a bit further than she did, we will perceive that it simply is not true that the governess gave such detailed descriptions of Peter Quint and Miss Jessel that Mrs. Grose instantly recognized their portraits. In the case of Miss Jessel, indeed, such a statement is the very reverse of the truth. The "detailed" description consisted, beyond the colorless fact that the ghost was pale, precisely of the two items that the woman who appeared was extremely beautiful and was dressed in black. But Mrs. Grose had already told the governess explicitly, long before any ghost was thought of, that Miss Jessel was beautiful. Whether she had been accustomed to dress in black we never learn. But that makes little difference, for the fact is that it is *the governess herself and not Mrs. Grose at all who does the identifying:*

> "Was she some one you've never seen?" asked Mrs. Grose.
>
> "Never," the governess replies. "But some one the child has. Some one *you* have." Then to show how I had thought it all out: "My predecessor—the one who died."
>
> "Miss Jessel?"
>
> "Miss Jessel," the governess confirms. "You don't believe me?"

And the ensuing conversation makes it abundantly plain that Mrs. Grose is still far from convinced. This seems a trifle odd in view of the fact that Peter Quint is known to be haunting the place. After having believed in one ghost, it ought not to be hard for Mrs. Grose to believe in another, especially when the human counterparts of the two were as inseparable in life as were the valet and the former governess. Which makes it look as if the housekeeper were perhaps not so certain after all in the case of Quint. Why, then, we ask, did she "identify him"? To which the answer is that she identified him because the suggestion for the identification, just as in the case of Miss Jessel, though much more subtly, comes from the governess herself. The skill with which James manages to throw the reader off the scent in this scene is consummate.

In the first place, the housekeeper herself, as we have had several occasions to remark, has already dropped an unintentional hint of someone in the neighborhood who preys on young and pretty governesses. This man, to be sure, is dead, but the new governess, who did not pay strict enough attention to Mrs. Grose's tenses, does not know it. We have already noted the part that the fear of him played in creating the figure on the tower. When now that figure comes closer and appears at the window, it would be strange indeed if, in turning over in her head all the possibilities, the idea of the unknown man to whom the housekeeper had so vaguely referred did not cross at least the fringe of the governess' consciousness. That it actually did is indicated by her prompt assumption that Mrs. Grose can identify their extraordinary visitor. "But now that you've guessed," are her words.

"Ah I haven't guessed," Mrs. Grose replies. And we are quite willing to agree that at this point she hasn't. But notice what follows:

The governess has assured Mrs. Grose that the intruder is not a gentleman.

"But if he isn't a gentleman—" the housekeeper begins.

"What *is* he?" asks the governess, completing the question and supplying the answer:

> "He's a horror."
>
> "A horror?"
>
> "He's—God help me if I know *what* he is!"
>
> Mrs. Grose looked round once more; she fixed her eyes on the duskier distance and then, pulling herself together, turned to me with full inconsequence. "It's time we should be at church."

What was the thought which was seeking entrance to Mrs. Grose's mind as she gazed at the duskier distance and which was sufficiently unwelcome to make her throw it off with her gesture and quick digression? Was it something that the word "horror" had suggested, something vaguely hinted in the governess's "He's—God help me if I know *what* he is!"—as if their visitant were a creature not altogether mortal? We cannot be sure. But when, immediately afterward, the governess refuses to go to church on the ground that the stranger is a menace to the *children,* there is no longer any question as to the thought that dawns over the housekeeper. *A horror in human form that is a menace to the children!* Is there anything, or anyone, in Mrs. Grose's experience that answers that description? A thousand times yes! Peter Quint. Can there be a shadow of doubt that it is Quint of whom she is thinking when, to use the author's words, her

> large face showed me, at this, for the first time, the far-away faint glimmer of a consciousness more acute: I somehow made out in it the delayed dawn of an idea I myself had not given her and that was as yet quite obscure to me. It comes back to me that I thought instantly of this as something I could get from her; and I felt it to be connected with the desire she presently showed to know more.

So do the governess' fears and repressed desires and the housekeeper's memories and anxieties unconsciously collaborate.

The conversation is resumed and the governess gives, in the most vivid detail, a picture of the man she has seen at the window. Following which, from the governess's challenge, "You *do* know him?" the housekeeper holds back for a second, only to admit, a moment later, that it is Peter Quint and to stagger her companion, in the next breath, by her calm declaration that Quint is dead.

Now with regard to all this the critical question is: Granted that Mrs. Grose's mind was already toying with the idea of Quint, how could she have identified him unless the governess' description tallied with the man? For, unlike Miss Jessel's, she has received no advance hint with regard to Quint's personal appearance, and the description, instead of being brief and generalized, is lengthy and concrete. The objection seems fatal to the view that the apparitions were mere creatures of the governess' imagination. But upon examination this line of argument will be found, I think, to prove too much.

Suppose a missing criminal is described as follows: "A squat, ruddy-cheeked man about thirty years old, weighing nearly two hundred pounds; thick lips and pockmarked face; one front tooth missing, two others with heavy gold fillings; big scar above left cheek bone. Wears shell glasses; had on, when last seen, brown suit, gray hat, pink shirt and tan shoes." Then suppose a man, flushed with excitement, were to rush into police headquarters exclaiming that he had found the murderer. "How do you know?" the chief detective asks. "Why! I saw a man about thirty years old with shell glasses and tan shoes!"

Well, it is only a slight exaggeration to say that Mrs. Grose's "identification" of Peter Quint, in the face of the governess' description, is of exactly this sort. The picture the latter draws of the face at the window, with its red curling hair and peculiar whiskers, is so vivid and striking that Mrs. Grose, if she was listening and if it was indeed a description of Quint, ought not to have hesitated a second. But she did hesitate. It may of course be said that she hesitated not because the description did not fit but because Quint was dead. But if so, why, when she does identify him, does she pick out the least characteristic points in the description? Why, when she does "piece it all together" (what irony in that "all"!), does her identification rest not at all on the red whiskers or the thin mouth, but, of all things, on the two facts that the stranger wore no hat and that his clothes looked as if they belonged to someone else? As if good ghosts always wore hats and bad ones carried their terrestrial pilferings into eternity! That touch about "the missing waistcoats" is precisely at Mrs. Grose's intellectual level, the level, as anyone who has ever had the curiosity to attend one knows, of a fifth-rate spiritualist seance.

The thing is really so absurd that we actually wonder whether Mrs. Grose was listening. Recall the beginning of the dialogue:

> "What's he like?" [asks Mrs. Grose]
> "I've been dying to tell you. But he's like nobody."
> "Nobody?" she echoed.
> "He has no hat." Then seeing in her face that she already, in this, with a deeper dismay, found a touch of picture, I quickly added stroke to stroke.

We see what we expect to see. That Mrs. Grose should so instantaneously find a touch of picture in the colorless item that "he had no hat" is a measure of the high degree of her suggestibility, as good proof as one could want that an image is already hovering in the background of her mind waiting to rush into the foreground at the faintest summons. That, as we have seen, is exactly what the image of Peter Quint is doing. And so, is it at all unlikely that in completing the picture of which the mention of the hat has supplied the first touch, Mrs. Grose pays scant attention to the other, verbal picture that the governess is drawing? The point need not be urged, but at any rate she gives no evidence of having heard, and at the governess' concluding sentence, "He gives me a sort of sense of looking like an actor," her echoed "An actor!" sounds almost as if it were at that point that her wandering attention were called back. That of course is only conjecture. But what is not conjecture, and significant enough, is the fact that the two shaky pegs on which Mrs. Grose hangs her identification come, one at the very beginning, the other at the very end, of a long description the intervening portions of which would have supplied her, any one of them, with solid support. When a man crosses a stream on a rotten wooden bridge in spite of the fact that there is a solid one of stone a rod or two away, you naturally wonder whether he has noticed it.

III

"But why waste so much breath," it will be said, "over what is after all such a purely preliminary part of the story and over such an incidental character as Mrs. Grose. Come to the main events, and to the central characters, the children. What *then* becomes of your theory that Quint and Miss Jessel are just hallucinations? How can they be that, when Miles and Flora see them?"

Before coming to this certainly pertinent objection, I wonder if I may interject the personal experience mentioned at the beginning. It may be that this experience subconsciously accounts for my reading of *The Turn of the Screw*. If its influence is justified, it is worth recounting. If it is unjustified, it should be narrated that the reader may properly discount its effect on my interpretation of the tale. It may be that for me this memory turns into realism what for even the author was only romance.

When I was a boy of seven or eight, and my sister a few years older, we had a servant in the family—a Canadian woman, I think she was—who, I now see on looking back (though no one then suspected it), was insane. Some years later her delusions became marked, her insanity was generally recognized, and she was for a time at least confined in an asylum. Now it happened that this woman, who was of an affectionate nature and loved children, used to tell us stories. I do not know whether they were all of one kind, but I do know that the only ones my memory retained were of dead people who came to visit her in the night. I remember with extraordinary vividness her account of a woman in white who came and stood silent at the foot of her bed. I can still see the strange smile—the insane smile, as I now recognize it to have been—that came over the face of the narrator as she told of this visitant. This woman did not long remain a servant in our family. But suppose she had! Suppose our parents had died, or, for some other reason, we had been placed exclusively in her care. (She was a woman of unimpeachable character and kindliest impulses.) What might have happened to us? What might not! Especially if she had conceived the notion that some of her spiritual visitants were of an infernal character and had come to gain possession of us, the children for whom she was responsible. I tremble to think. And yet no greater alteration than this would have been called for in an instance within the range of my own experience to have duplicated essentially what I conceive to be the situation in *The Turn of the Screw*.

Now the unlikelihood of this situation's occurring is precisely the fact that in real life someone would recognize the insanity and interfere to save the children. This was the difficulty that confronted the author of *The Turn of the Screw*, if we may assume for the moment that I have stated his problem correctly. The extraordinary skill and thoroughness with which he has met it are themselves the proof, it seems to me, that he had that difficulty very consciously in his mind. He overcomes it by fashioning the characters of the master and the housekeeper expressly to fit the situation. The children's uncle, from the first, wishes to wash his hands entirely of their upbringing, to put them unreservedly in the hands of their governess, who is *never,* in any conceivable way, to put up her problems or questions to him in person or by letter. The insistence on this from beginning to end seems needlessly emphatic unless it serves some such purpose as the one indicated. The physical isolation of the little household in the big estate at Bly is also complete. The governess is in supreme authority; only she and the housekeeper have anything to do with the children—and Mrs. Grose's character is shaped to fit the plot. If she is the incarnation of practical household sense and homely affection, she is utterly devoid of worldly experience and imagination. And she is as superstitious as such a person is likely to be. She can neither read nor write, the latter fact, which is a capital one, being especially insisted on. She knows her place and has a correspondingly exalted opinion of persons of higher rank or education. Hence her willingness, even when she cannot understand, to accept as truth whatever the governess tells her. She loves the children deeply and has suffered terribly for them during the reign of Quint and Miss Jessel. (Her relief on the arrival of Miss Jessel's successor, which the latter notices and misinterprets, is natural.) Here is a character, then, and a situation, ideally fitted to allow of the development of the governess' mania unnoticed. James speaks of the original suggestion for *The Turn of the Screw* as "the vividest little note for sinister romance that I had ever jotted down," expressing wonder at the same time "why so fine a germ, gleaming there in the wayside dust of life, had never been deftly picked up." His note, he says in one of his letters, was "of a most scrappy kind." The form which the idea assumed in his mind as it developed we can only conjecture. My own guess would be that it might, in content at least, have run something like this: *Two children, under circumstances where there is no one to realize the situation, are put, for bringing up, in the care of an insane governess.*

IV

With this hypothesis as a clue, we can trace the art with which James hypnotizes us into forgetting that it is the governess' version of the story to which we are listening, and lures us, as the governess unconsciously lured Mrs. Grose, into accepting her coloring of the facts for the facts themselves.

It is solely on the governess' say-so that we agree to the notion that the two specters have returned in search of the *children.* Again it is on her unsupported word that we accept for fact her statement that, on the occasion in the garden when Miss Jessel first appeared, Flora *saw*. The scene itself, after Miss Jessel's advent, is not presented. (Time enough to present his scenes when James has "suggested" to his readers what they shall see.) What happened is narrated by the governess, who simply announces flatly to Mrs. Grose that, "Two hours ago, in the garden, Flora *saw*." And when Mrs. Grose naturally enough demands, ". . . how do you know?" her only answer is, "I was there —I saw with my eyes," an answer valuable or worthless in direct proportion to the governess' power to see things as they are.

In the case of Miles the method is the same except that James, feeling that he now has a grip on the reader, proceeds more boldly. The scene is not narrated this time; it is presented—but only indirectly. The governess, looking down from a window, catches Miles out at midnight on the lawn. He gazes up, as nearly as she can figure, to a point on the building over her head. Whereupon she promptly draws the inference: "There was clearly another person above me— there was a person on the tower." This, when we stop to think, is even "thinner" than in the case of Flora and Miss Jessel, for this time even the governess does not see, she merely infers. The boy gazes up. "Clearly" there was a man upon the tower. That "clearly" lets the cat out of the bag. It shows, as every tyro in psychology should know, that "clear" is precisely what the thing is not.

These two instances are typical of the governess' mania. She seizes the flimsiest pretexts for finding confirmation of her suspicions. Her theories swell to such immense dimensions that when the poor little facts emerge they are immediately swallowed up. She half admits this to herself at the very beginning of the story: "It seems to me indeed, in raking it all over," she says of the night following the appearance of Quint at the dining room window, "that by the time the morrow's sun was high I had restlessly read into the facts before us almost all the meaning they were to receive from subsequent and more cruel occurrences." Scarcely ever was the essence of mania better compressed into a sentence than in her statement: "The more I go over it the more I see in it, and the more I see in it the more I fear. I don't know what I *don't* see, what I *don't* fear!" Or again, where in speaking of the children's lessons and her conversations with them she says:

> All roads lead to Rome, and there were times when it might have struck us that almost every branch of study or subject of conversation skirted forbidden ground. Forbidden ground was the question of the return of the dead in general and of whatever, in especial, might survive, for memory, of the friends little children had lost. There were days when I could have sworn that one of them had, with a small invisible nudge, said to the other: "She thinks she'll do it this time—but she won't!" To "do it" would have been to indulge for instance—and for once in a way

—in some direct reference to the lady who had prepared them for my discipline.

And from this she goes on to the conviction that the children have fallen into the habit of entertaining Quint and Miss Jessel unknown to her.

> "There were times of our being together when I would have been ready to swear that, literally, in my presence, but with my direct sense of it closed, they had visitors who were known and were welcome. Then it was that, had I not been deterred by the very chance that such an injury might prove greater than the injury to be averted, my exaltation would have broken out. "They're here, they're here, you little wretches," I would have cried, "and you can't deny it now!"

Her proof in these cases, it will be noted, is the fact that she "could have sworn" that it was so.

How completely innocent and natural the children really were through all these earlier passages of the drama anyone will see who will divest himself of the suggestion that the governess has planted in his mind. The pranks they play are utterly harmless, and when she questions the perpetrators, because they are perfectly truthful, they have the readiest and most convincing answers at hand. Why did little Miles get up in the middle of the night and parade out on the lawn? Just as he said, in order that, for once, she might think him *bad.* Why did Flora rise from her bed at the same hour? By agreement with Miles. Why did she gaze out the window? To disturb her governess and make her look too. These answers, true every one, ought to have disarmed the children's inquisitor. But she has her satanic hypothesis, so that the very readiness of their replies convicts instead of acquitting them in her eyes. They are inspired answers, she holds, splendidly but diabolically inspired. They scintillate with a mental power beyond the children's years. "Their more than earthly beauty, their absolutely unnatural goodness. It's a game," she cries, "it's a policy and a fraud!"

And the same is true of the children's conversation as of their conduct. Always their remarks are direct and ingenuous; always she reads into them an infernal meaning—until, when she says of Miles, ". . . horrible as it was his lies made up my truth," we see that the exact reverse of this is the case: that in reality his truth, and Flora's, made up her lies. If Miles asks about "this queer business of ours," meaning the queer way his education is being attended to, she takes it as referring to the boy's queer intercourse with Quint. If, when she remarks to Miles that they are alone, the latter replies that they still have "the others," obviously referring to the servants, the governess is not content to take his words at their face value but must interpret "the others" as referring to the specters. So candid, so unsophisticated, so prompt are the children's answers that even the governess' insane conviction at times seems shaken. But always—so James contrives it—some convenient bit of *objective* evidence comes in to reassure her: the fearful language that Flora uses in her delirium, the boy's lie about the letter, the clear evidence at the end that he has something on his mind that he longs to confess.

As these last examples suggest, it is necessary to qualify the idea that Miles and Flora are just happy natural children. They are that during the earlier passages of the story. But they do not continue to be. And the change is brought about by no one but the governess herself. Herein lies one of the subtlest aspects of the story.

Fear is like faith: it ultimately creates what at first it only imagined. The governess, at the beginning, imagines that the actions and words of the children are strange and unnatural. In the end they become strange and unnatural for the good and sufficient reason that the children gradually become conscious of the strangeness and unnaturalness of her own attitude toward them. They cannot put it into words: they have never heard of nervousness, still less of insanity. But they sense it and grow afraid, and she accepts the abnormal condition into which their fear of *her* has thrown them as proof of their intercourse with the two specters. Thus do her mania and their fear feed and augment each other, until the situation culminates—in a preliminary way—in two scenes of shuddering terror.

The first of these is the occasion when the governess comes at night to Miles's bedside and tries, without mentioning the dreaded name of Quint, to wring from the child a confession of the infernal intercourse which, she is convinced, he is guilty of holding. Forget, for the moment, the governess' version of the occurrence and think of it as it must have appeared to the child. A little boy of ten, who has for some time felt something creepy and uncanny in the woman who has been placed in charge of him and his sister, lies awake in the dark thinking of her and of the strangeness of it all. He hears steps outside his door. At his call the door opens, and there, candle in hand, is this very woman. She enters and sits beside him on the edge of the bed. For a moment or two she talks naturally, asking him why he is not asleep. He tells her. And then, quite suddenly, he notices in her voice the queer tone he has felt before, and the something in her manner, excited but suppressed, that he does not like. As they go on talking, this excitement grows and grows, until in a final outburst she falls on her knees before him and begs him to let her *save* him! Visualize the scene: the hapless child utterly at a loss to know what the dreadful "something" is from which she would "save" him; the insane woman on her knees almost clasping him in her hysterical embrace. Is it any wonder that the interview terminates in a shriek that bursts from the lips of the terror-stricken boy? Nothing could be more natural. Yet, characteristically, the governess interprets the boy's fright and outcry as convincing proof of the presence of the creature she is seeking to exorcise. Utterly unconscious of the child's fear of *her,* she attributes his agitation to the only other adequate cause she can conceive.

The corresponding scene in the case of Flora occurs the next day by the lake. Once more, think of it from the angle of the child. A little girl, too closely watched and confined by her governess, seizes an opportunity for freedom that presents itself and wanders off for half an hour in the grounds of the estate where she lives. A little later, the governess and the housekeeper, out of breath with searching, come upon her. A half-dozen words have hardly been exchanged when the governess, a tremor in her voice, turns suddenly on the child and demands to know where her former governess is—a woman whom the little girl knows perfectly well is dead and buried. The child's face blanches, the housekeeper utters a cry, in answer to which the governess, pointing across the lake and into vacancy cries out: "She's there, she's there!" The child stares at the demented woman in consternation. The latter repeats: "She's there, you little unhappy thing —there, there, *there,* and you know it as well as you know me!" The little girl holding fast to the housekeeper, is frozen in a convulsion of fear. She recovers herself sufficiently to cry out, "I don't know what you mean. I see nobody. I see nothing. I never *have,*" and then, hiding her head in the housekeeper's skirts, she breaks out in a wail, "Take me away, take me away—oh take me away from *her!*"

"From *me?*" the governess cries, as if thunderstruck that it is not from the specter that she asks to be delivered.

"From you—from you!" the child confirms.

Again, is not the scene, when innocently taken, perfectly natural? Yet again the governess is incapable of perceiving that the child is stricken with terror not at all at the apparition but at *her* and the effect the apparition has had upon her.

V

"All of which is very clever and might be very convincing," it will be promptly objected, "if it did not calmly leave out of account the paramount fact of the whole narrative, that in the end Miles *does* see and identifies Quint by name. It was this "supreme surrender of the name" that justified and redeemed the governess' devotion. Never, never—it was a point of honor—had the name of Quint crossed her lips in Miles's presence. When, then, it crossed his lips in her presence, it was the long sought proof that from the first he had been holding communication with the spirit of the dead man. That is the very point and climax of the story."

If you think so, you have failed to trace the chain of causation down which the name of Peter Quint vibrates from the brain of the governess to the lips of little Miles.[1] True, it was a point of honor with her not to breathe the name of Quint in the children's presence. But how about the name of Quint's companion? Ought not silence with regard to Miss Jessel's to have been equally sacred? It surely should have been. But there, it will be remembered, the governess' self-control failed her. On that day, by the lake, when, as we have seen, she blurted out to Flora her fatal, "Where, my pet, is Miss Jessel?" only to answer her own question a second later by gazing into what to the two others was vacancy and shrieking, "She's there, she's there!" she fixed forever in the child's mind a bond between her own (that is, the governess') strange "possession" and the name of Miss Jessel.

Flora, as we have remarked, is driven half out of her senses with fright, and while she has never "seen" Miss Jessel previously, nothing is more probable than that she "sees" her now. At the very least, memories of her and of the time the child was in her care figure prominently in the delirium that follows the shock of witnessing the governess' strange affliction. Whatever Flora's feelings toward her former governess originally were, from now on they will be linked inextricably with her fear of her present one. The two are merged in a single complex. How do we know? Because the child, in her delirium, uses shocking language or ideas which she has picked up in the days when Miss Jessel consorted with Peter Quint. To poor Mrs. Grose this is, at last, final proof that the governess is right in suspecting the little girl of diabolical intercourse. To the reader it ought to be proof of nothing of the sort. Nearly everyone remembers the case of the ignorant maidservant of the Hebrew scholar who, on being hypnotized, would overflow in a torrent of extraordinarily fluent Hebrew. This gift came very far from proving her learned in Hebrew. Quite as little did the "horrors," to use Mrs. Grose's word, to which Flora gives utterance in her fever prove her a depraved or vicious child. An interesting parallel and variant of the same motive is found in the innocent profanity of Hareton Earnshaw in *Wuthering Heights*, verbally shocking language from the lips of a rarely beautiful character.

The next link in the chain is the fact that Miles sees Flora between

[1] For I do not think we are entitled to infer that Miles learned anything from the stolen letter.

the time she is taken ill and the scene of his final interview with the governess. The very brevity of the author's reference to this fact suggests his expectation that the breathless or unwary reader will read right over it without getting its significance. (If it has no significance, why mention it at all?) The governess, fearing that Flora, who has now turned against her, will influence Miles to do the same, warns Mrs. Grose against giving her the opportunity to do so.

> "There's one thing, of course" [she says]: "they mustn't, before she goes, see each other for three seconds." Then it came over me that, in spite of Flora's presumable sequestration from the instant of her return from the pool, it might already be too late. "Do you mean," I anxiously asked, "that they *have* met?"
>
> At this she quite flushed. "Ah, Miss, I'm not such a fool as that! If I've been obliged to leave her three or four times, it has been each time with one of the maids, and at present, though she's alone, she's locked in safe. And yet—and yet!" There were too many things.
>
> "And yet what?"

Mrs. Grose never really answers this "And yet what?" which, together with her flushing when the governess asks her if the children have met, more than intimates that they already have, especially in view of the assumed complete trustworthiness of "the maids." That they do meet later, at any rate, we know from half a sentence thrown in with seeming inadvertence in the next chapter. Vague as the matter is left, it is clear that the boy had an opportunity to fix in his mind a connection between his sister's illness, her dread of their present governess, and—Miss Jessel. It was an uncomprehended connection to be sure, but its effect on the boy's mind must have been all the more powerful on that account—and the more so at this particular moment because under the stress of the governess' attempt to extort a confession from him his mind was already magnifying his venial fault about the letter into a mortal sin.

When, then, at the end, the governess in the presence of her hallucination shrieks to Peter Quint that he shall possess her boy "No more, no more, no more!" and the child, panting in her insane embrace, realizes that she sees someone at the window, how natural, how inevitable, that he should ask if "she" is *"here,"* and to the echoed question of the governess, who this "she" is, should reply, "Miss Jessel, Miss Jessel!" Bear in mind that, all through, it is Miss Jessel, according to the governess, who has been visiting Flora, while it is Quint who has been holding communication with Miles. Why, if the boy has been in the habit of consorting with the spirit of Quint and if he senses now the nearness of a ghostly visitant, why, I say, does he not ask if *he* is here? Surely, then, his "Is *she* here?" is the best possible proof that the idea of a spiritual presence has been suggested not at all by past experiences of a similar sort but precisely by something he has overheard from Flora, or about her, plus what he gets at the moment from the governess.

"I seized, stupified, his supposition," she says, at his utterance of Miss Jessel's name, "—some sequel to what we had done to Flora, but this made me only want to show him that it was better still than that." (In one flash that "better" lays bare the governess' possession!) "It's not Miss Jessel!" she goes on. "But it's at the window—straight before us. It's *there,* the coward horror, there for the last time!"

If we could hear her voice when she cries, "It's not Miss Jessel!" I suspect that her intonation of the last two words would show how completely, if unconsciously, she conveyed *to* the boy's mind the very name which her whole justification depended on receiving *from* him. The child's next question, "It's *he?*" is but an ellipsis for "If, then, it is not *she,* you mean it must be the other one of the two who were always together?" But the governess, determined not to be the first to mention the unmentionable name, demands, "Whom do you mean by 'he'?"

"Peter Quint—you devil!" is the child's reply in words that duplicate, more briefly and even more tragically, the psychology of the "horrors" uttered by his sister in her delirium. But even now he does not see, though he accepts the governess' assurance that Peter Quint is there. *"Where?"* he cries. And that last word his lips ever utter, as his eye roams helplessly about the room in a vain endeavor to *see,* gives the ultimate lie to the notion that he does see now or has ever seen. But the governess, deluded to the end, takes it as meaning that at last the horror is exorcised and the child himself dispossessed.

VI

If on your first reading of *The Turn of the Screw* the hypothesis did not occur to you that the governess is insane, run through the story again and you will hardly know which to admire more, James's daring in introducing the cruder physical as distinguished from the subtler psychological symptoms of insanity or his skill in covering them up and seeming to explain them away. The insane woman is telling her own story. She cannot see her own insanity—she can only see its reflection, as it were, in the faces, trace its effect on the acts, of others. And because "the others" are in her case children and an ignorant and superstitious woman, these reflections and effects are to be found in the sphere of their emotions rather than in that of their understandings. They see and feel her insanity, but they cannot comprehend or name it.

The most frequent mark of her disease is her insane *look* which is mirrored for us in the countenances and eyes of the others.

Mrs. Grose first sees this look in something like its fullness when the governess gazes through the window of the dining room after she has seen Peter Quint. So terrible is the sight of her face that Mrs. Grose draws back blanched and stunned, quite as if it were a ghost that she had seen. "Did I look very queer?" the governess asks a moment later when the housekeeper has joined her. "Through this window?" Mrs. Grose returns. "Dreadful!"

There are a dozen other passages that strike the same note:

"I was conscious as I spoke that I looked prodigious things," says the governess, "for I got the slow reflection of them in my companion's face."

"Ah with such awful eyes!" she exclaims in another passage, referring to the way Miss Jessel fixed her gaze on Flora. Whereupon, she continues, Mrs. Grose "stared at mine as if they might really have resembled them." And a moment later: "Mrs. Grose—her eyes just lingering on mine—gave a shudder and walked to the window."

In a later conversation between the same two: "I don't wonder you looked queer," says the governess, "when I mentioned to you the letter from his school!" "I doubt if I looked as queer as you!" the housekeeper retorts.

"I remember that, to gain time, I tried to laugh," the governess writes of her walk to church with Miles, "and I seemed to see in the beautiful face with which he watched me how ugly and queer I looked."

To which should be added the passage, too long to quote, in which Flora recognizes for the first time the full "queerness" of her governess, the passage that culminates in her agonized cry: "Take me away, take me away—oh take me away from *her!*"

The governess' insane laugh, as well as her insane look, is frequently alluded to. Of this we have just mentioned one example. Of references to her maniacal cries there are several: "I had to smother a kind of howl," she says when Mrs. Grose tells her of Quint's relations with the children. Or again, when she catches Miss Jessel sitting at her table: "I heard myself break into a sound that, by the open door, rang through the long passage and the empty house." What do we say of persons who shriek in empty houses—or who frighten children into similar outbreaks? "The boy gave a loud high shriek which, lost in the rest of the shock of sound, might have seemed, indistinctly, though I was so close to him, a note either of jubilation or of terror."

The wonder is not that the children cried out, but that they did not cry out sooner or oftener. "I must have gripped my little girl with a spasm that, wonderfully, she submitted to without a cry or a sign of fright." The implications of that sentence prepare us for the scene in Miles's bedchamber where the governess falls on her knees before the boy and for the final scene where she locks him in her insane embrace.

But the psychological symptoms are more interesting than the more obviously physical ones.

The consciousness of the governess that she is skirting the brink of the abyss is especially significant. It reminds us of Lear's: "That way madness lies." Only in her case we have to take her word for it that she never goes over the edge.

"We were to keep our heads," she says, "if we should keep nothing else—difficult indeed as that might be. . . ."

"I began to watch them in a stifled suspense," she remarks of the children, "a disguised tension, that might well, had it continued too long, have turned to something like madness. What saved me, as I now see, was that it turned to another matter altogether." Of the truth of this last assertion the governess presents precisely nothing but her own word as proof. Or, to put it from her own angle, she presents—the apparitions. "She was there," she says of Miss Jessel's appearance by the lake, "so I was justified; she was there, so I was neither cruel nor mad." The irony of summoning a specter as witness that one is not mad is evident enough.

Indeed this style of reasoning does not quite satisfy the governess herself in her more normal intervals. There are moments throughout the tale when a lurking doubt of her own sanity comes to the surface. When, for instance, Mrs. Grose begs her to write to the master and explain their predicament, she turns on her with the question whether she can write him that his little niece and nephew are mad. "But if they *are,* Miss?" says Mrs. Grose. "And if I am myself, you mean?" the governess retorts. And when she is questioning Miles, on the very edge of the final catastrophe, the same paralyzing thought floats for a second into her consciousness: ". . . if he *were* innocent what then on earth was I?" That she never succeeded in utterly banishing this terrible hypothesis is shown by the view of the case she takes long after the events are over and she is writing her account of them: "It was not," she sets it down, "I am as sure to-day as I was sure then, my mere infernal imagination." Clear proof that she was sure at neither time.

There are a dozen other passages, if there were only space to quote them, that show how penetratingly, if unconsciously, the sane remnant of the governess' nature can diagnose her own case and comprehend the character of the two apparitions. "What arrested me on the spot," she says of the figure on the tower, ". . . was the sense that my imagination had, in a flash, turned real." "There were shrubberies and big trees," she says when she is hunting for Quint on the lawn, "but

I remember the clear assurance I felt that none of them concealed him. He was there or was not there: not there if I didn't see him." The account of the first appearance of Miss Jessel, too, if read attentively, reveals clearly the psychological origin of the apparition, as does the governess' account of the experience, later, to Mrs. Grose:

> "I was there with the child—quiet for the hour; and in the midst of it she came."
>
> "Came how—from where?"
>
> "From where they come from! She just appeared and stood there—but not so near."
>
> "And without coming nearer?"
>
> "Oh for the effect and the feeling she might have been as close as you!"

But perhaps the most interesting and convincing point in this whole connection is the fact that the appearance of the ghosts is timed to correspond not at all with some appropriate or receptive moment in the children's experience but very nicely with some mental crisis in the governess'. In the end their emergence is a signal, as it were, of a further loss of self-control on her part, an advance in her mania. "Where, my pet, is Miss Jessel?" she asks Flora, committing the tragic indiscretion of mentioning the interdicted name. And presto! Miss Jessel appears. "Tell me," she says, pressing Miles cruelly to the wall in their last interview, "if, yesterday afternoon, from the table in the hall, you took, you know, my letter." And instantly Peter Quint comes into view "like a sentinel before a prison." But the last instance of all is the most revealing. With the ruthlessness of an inquisitor she has extorted from Miles the confession that he "said things" at school. It is not enough that he tells her to whom he said them. She must follow it up to the bitter end. "What *were* these things?" she demands unpardonably. Whereupon, "again, against the glass, as if to blight his confession and stay his answer, was the hideous author of our woe—the white face of damnation." If perfect synchronization is any criterion, surely, with these instances before us, the inference is inescapable that if Peter Quint has come out of the grave to infect or capture anyone, it is the governess and not the child.

VII

There will doubtless be those who can quite agree with all I have said about *The Turn of the Screw* who will nevertheless not thank me for saying it. "Here was the one ghost story left," they will protest, "that carried a genuine mystery in it. And you proceed to rationalize it ruthlessly, to turn it, in James's own words, into a 'mere modern "psychical" case, washed clean of all queerness as by exposure to a flowing laboratory tap.' What a pity!"

But do I rationalize it, ruthlessly or otherwise? Is insanity something easier to probe and get to the bottom of than a crude spiritualism? Are Peter Quint and Miss Jessel a whit less mysterious or less appalling because they are evoked by the governess's imagination? Are they a whit less real? Surely the human brain is as solid a fact as the terrestrial globe, and inhabitants of the former have just as authentic an existence as inhabitants of the latter. Nor do I mean by that to imply, as to some I will seem to have implied all through, that Peter Quint and Miss Jessel exist *only* in the brain of the governess. Perhaps they do and perhaps they don't. Like Hawthorne in similar situations—but with an art that makes even Hawthorne look clumsy—James is wise enough and intellectually humble enough to leave that question open. Nobody knows enough about insanity yet to be dogmatic on such a matter. Whether the insane man creates his hallucinations or whether insanity is precisely the power to perceive objective existences of another order, whether higher or lower, than humanity, no open-minded person can possibly pretend to say, however preponderating in the one direction or the other present evidence may seem to him to be. Whoever prefers to, then, is free to believe that the governess sees the actual spirits of Peter Quint and Miss Jessel. Nothing in the tale, I have tried to show, demands that hypothesis. But nothing, on the other hand, absolutely contradicts it. Indeed, there is room between these extremes for a third possibility. Perhaps the governess' brain caught a true image of Peter Quint straight from Mrs. Grose's memory via the ether or some subtler medium of thought transference. The tale in these respects is susceptible of various readings. But for one theory it offers, I hold, not an inch of standing ground: for the idea, namely, that the children *saw*.

This is the crucial point. Everything else is incidental. Believe that the children saw, and the tale is one thing. Believe that they did not see, and it is another—as different as light from darkness. Either way the story is one of the most powerful ever written. But in the former event it is merely dreadful. In the latter it is dreadful, but also beautiful. One way, it is a tale of corrupted childhood. The other, it is a tale of incorruptible childhood. Of the two, can it be doubted which it is? Miles and Flora are touched, it is true, by the evil of Peter Quint and Miss Jessel, but they are not tainted. That evil leaves its mark, if you will, but no trace of stain or smirch. The children remain what they were—incarnations of loveliness and charm. Innocence is armor plate: that is what the story seems to say. And does not life bear out that belief? Otherwise, in what but infamy would the younger generation ever end? Miles and Flora, to be sure, are withered at last in the flame of the governess' passion. But corrupted—never! And the withering of them in the flame is rendered tragic rather than merely horrible by the heroism that they display. The things that children suffer in silence! Because, as here, their heroism generally takes the form of endurance rather than of daring, rarely, if ever, in literature or in life, is justice done to the incredible, the appalling courage of childhood. This story does do justice to it.

But in stressing the courage of the children, we must not pass over the same quality in the governess. That is clear enough however we read the tale. But her courage gets an added value, if we accept her mental condition as abnormal, from the fact of its showing the shallowness of the prevailing notion that insanity inevitably betokens a general breakdown of the higher faculties. It may mean that. But it may not. No small part of the horror and tragedy of our treatment of the insane flows from our failure to realize that mental aberration may go hand in hand with strength and beauty of character. It does in this case. The governess is deluded, but she rises to the sublime in her delusion.

The tale clarifies certain of the causes of insanity also. The hereditary seed of the disease in this instance is hinted at in the one reference to the young woman's father. And her environment was precisely the right one for its germination. The reaction upon a sensitive and romantic nature of the narrowness of English middle class life in the last century: that, from the social angle, is the theme of the story. The sudden change of scene, the sudden immense responsibility placed on unaccustomed shoulders, the shock of sudden unrequited affection—all these together—were too much. The brain gives way. And what follows is a masterly tracing of the effects of repressed love and thwarted maternal affection. The whole story might be reviewed with profit under this psychoanalytic aspect. But when it was done, less would probably have been conveyed than James packs into a single simile. He throws it out, with seeming nonchalance, during the governess's last interview, after Flora's delirium, with little Miles:

> Our meal was of the briefest—mine a vain pretense, and I had the things immediately removed. While this was done Miles stood again with his hands in his little pockets and his back to me—stood and looked out of the wide window through which, that other day, I had seen what pulled me up. We continued silent while the maid was with us—as silent, it whimsically occurred to me, as some young couple who, on their wedding-journey, at the inn, feel shy in the presence of the waiter.

The simile strikes the governess as whimsical. Whimsical in reality is precisely what it is not, guiding us, as it does, straight into her soul and plucking out the mystery of her lacerated heart.

VIII

If anyone will take the trouble to read, in the letters of Henry James, all the passages referring to *The Turn of the Screw,* I shall be surprised if he does not come away with the impression—which at any rate is emphatically mine—of a very charming and good-humored, but a nonetheless very unmistakable, side-stepping of questions or comments which had evidently been flung at him, touching his "bogey-tale," as he calls it, by H. G. Wells, F. W. H. Myers, and at least one other correspondent—a side-stepping to the effectiveness of which, without risk of offense to its victims, James's peculiar style was not less than gloriously adapted. He consistently deprecates his tale as a "very mechanical matter . . . an inferior, a merely *pictorial,* subject, and rather a shameless potboiler." The element of truth in this is obvious. We need not question James's sincerity. But in the face of the long list of notable critics and readers who, with different turns of phrase, have characterized *The Turn of the Screw* as one of the most powerful things ever written, it will not do to dismiss it as a mere exercise in literary ingenuity. It is easier to believe either that the author had a reason for belittling it or that his genius builded better than he knew. And indeed when we read his comment on the tale in the preface to the twelfth volume of his collected works, we see that he had come, partly perhaps under the pressure of its reception, which clearly exceeded his "liveliest hope," to put a somewhat higher estimate on his quondam "potboiler." He still speaks of it as a piece of "cold artistic calculation" deliberately planned "to catch those not easily caught (the 'fun' of the capture of the merely witless being ever but small), the jaded, the disillusioned, the fastidious." But in the retrospect he does not disguise his satisfaction with the tale or his sense of having struggled successfully with its technical difficulties and dangers. "Droll enough," he confesses, referring to letters received after its publication, was some of the testimony to that success. He tells of one reader in particular "capable evidently, for the time, of some attention, but not quite capable of enough," who complained that he hadn't sufficiently " 'characterized' " the governess. What wonder that the author's "ironic heart," as he puts it, "shook for the instant almost to breaking," under the reproach of not having sufficiently characterized a figure to the penetrating and detailed setting forth of whose mental condition every sentence of the story (barring part of the brief introductory chapter), from the first one to the last, is dedicated! "We have surely as much of her own nature as we can swallow," he writes in answer to this critic, "in watching it reflect her anxieties and inductions." He speaks of the necessity of having the governess keep "crystalline her record of so many intense anomalies and obscurities," and then adds, "—by which I don't of course mean her explanation of them, a different matter."

Now whether these various references to catching "those not easily caught," to the "droll" evidence of the success of his "ingenuity," to his "ironic heart" that "shook for the instant almost to breaking" under the reproaches of readers incapable of quite enough attention, whether all of these things, coupled with the clear, if casual, warning that the governess's "explanation" of her experiences is a "different matter" from a clear record of them, have any separate or cumulative significance, I will not pretend to say. In even hinting at anything of the sort, I may be guilty of twisting perfectly innocent statements to fit a hypothesis. They do appear to fit with curiously little stretching. But I do not press the point. It is not vital. It in no way affects the main argument. For in these matters it is always the work itself and not the author that is the ultimate authority.

Imagination and Time in "The Beast in the Jungle"

by Elisabeth Hansot

In his preface to *Joseph Andrews,* Maynard Mack suggests that the comic artist achieves his effect by subordinating the presentation of life as experience to the presentation of life as a spectacle. In the first instance the relationship between the characters experiencing life and the reader is a primary one, whereas in the second instance the characters remain detached from the events they observe and the primary relationship of reader and characters is that of onlookers.[1]

"The Beast in the Jungle" is not a comedy but its central character, Marcher, can nonetheless be described in Mack's terms. Marcher is a person who chooses to experience life as a spectacle. Consequently, the only relationship that Marcher can offer May is that of an onlooker, albeit a privileged one with access to information withheld from "the amusement of a cold world." [2] The reader, to reverse Mack's terms, is invited to figure to himself, through Marcher, the quality of life that can result from holding ordinary experience at arm's length.

Marcher's detachment from ordinary experience, James tells us, comes from his conviction that an extraordinary experience awaits him which, like a supernatural event, is expected to dislocate, supersede, or render meaningless the normal incidents and attitudes which make up a good part of everyday life. In the course of his narrative James describes some of the attitudes and beliefs which enable Marcher to establish and maintain a distance between himself and the everyday experience available to him, and suggests how, in turn, these disposi-

---

[1] Henry Fielding, *Joseph Andrews,* ed. Maynard Mack (New York: Holt, Rinehart, and Winston, 1948), p. xv.

[2] *The Complete Tales of Henry James,* ed. Leon Edel, 12 vols. (New York: J. B. Lippincott Company, 1964), XI, 363. All references to "The Beast in the Jungle" are from this edition and will be cited subsequently in parentheses after quotations in the text.

tions come to constitute the substance of Marcher's own character. One of the most noteworthy concomitants of Marcher's detachment is the curiously passive attitude he adopts toward his own past and future. This passivity—whether it be a cause or a consequence of his detachment—has among its effects a gradual and unperceived impoverishment of his own sensibility, for Marcher maintains toward his own past and future the attitude of a spectator viewing events that he cannot influence. He seems to view both these dimensions of time as discrete, self-contained objects, endowed with their own independent value and bearing little or no relationship to himself in the present.

When Marcher does try to conceive of himself as an active agent he chooses the paradigm of the hero. The hero's singularity might be said to consist in his ability to dominate events by his perfectly timed and conceived actions. James describes this kind of abrupt shift in Marcher's concept of himself as a sudden passage from one extreme of consciousness to another. (364) The images James uses to portray Marcher's rapid, almost unconscious transitions from passive spectator to heroic actor offer important clues to Marcher's attitude toward time.

In his opening sentence, James indicates that Marcher is not interested in questions of causality. "What determined the speech that startled him in the course of their encounter scarcely matters, being probably but some words spoken by himself quite without intention. . . . (351) Marcher at this juncture is wondering what had brought May to remind him of a long forgotten intimacy, a confession made to her ten years ago. Both the past confession and the present rediscovery of it appear to be fortunate accidents, explained, if explanation is needed, by some words spoken by Marcher without intent or purpose. Marcher seems to be a man to whom accidents—including accidents of memory—occur easily. As James portrays him, both in his initial setting at Weatherend and subsequently, Marcher does not conceive of himself as an active agent capable of initiating changes or causing events to occur in his everyday world. He is a man who lacks intentions, perhaps because he lacks desires and purposes by which to define himself and furnish his corner of the universe.

When Marcher does look to the past, it is because he desires to find a groundwork strong enough to support further intimacy with May in the future. He had, James remarks, most curiously forgotten the events of their encounter. The explanation may be that for Marcher these events seemed, in the strongest sense of the word, to be mere accidents, episodes which did not mark him, or even annoy or amuse him enough to recollect them in the intervening years. Marcher's past, seen in this light, might be described as a collection of incidents without continuity or form. These incidents appear as finished, somewhat gratuitous episodes, with little relation to the present and fewer implications for the future.

> . . . He was still merely fumbling with the idea that any contact between them in the past would have had no importance. If it had had no importance he scarcely knew why his actual impression of her should so seem to have so much; the answer to which, however, was that in such a life as they all appeared to be leading for the moment one could but take things as they came. (352)

Another way of describing what has happened to Marcher is to say he declines to live in ordinary time—the time in which people fall in love, get married, assume responsibilities, acquire possessions, and, like the visitors to Weatherend, long for others they cannot acquire. Quite to the contrary, Marcher's concern, upon becoming reacquainted with May, is that she show no right or claim to him.

> The vanity of women had long memories, but she was making no claim on him of a compliment or a mistake. With another woman, a totally different one, he might have feared the recall possibly even of some imbecile "offer." (356)

While he does obscurely sense that something will be required of him if the present meeting with May is to contain the germ for the future development, when Marcher reaches out it is only "in imagination—as against time" that he chooses to look for a fresh start. (356)

Why does James speak of "imagination as *against* time?" As James uses the idea of imagination the phrase implies that Marcher still has available to him a choice of roots by which he can try to reestablish his acquaintance with May. Marcher prefers to use his imagination, James suggests, because the humdrum activity, the everyday business of life, encountered on the alternative route seems trivial to him. But as Marcher himself ages and the unused and disdained possibilities of experience within ordinary time are withdrawn, Marcher's imagination comes to serve as a weapon to preserve himself against time.

> "Only, you know, it isn't anything I'm to *do,* to achieve in the world, to be distinguished or admired for. I'm not such an ass as *that.*" (359–60)[3]

As the time alloted him diminishes, Marcher's refusal to seriously take in hand and give value to the everyday business of life makes him dangerously dependent upon the existence of his singular fate, the occurrence of which will, presumably, both vindicate his attitude to-

[3] One might speculate that Marcher chooses to remain detached from possible experiences just because they appear to him to be common, in the sense of being available to everyone. However, their common character, as has been suggested, may be said to exist only so long as Marcher refuses to make the experiences his own—to give them the imprint of his own wants and needs.

ward ordinary time and redeem the insignificance of his present life. And, as the margin of time shrinks, Marcher's anxiety increases. He becomes aware that "when the possibilities themselves had accordingly turned stale, when the secret of the gods had grown faint, had perhaps even quite evaporated that, and that only, was failure." (379) But even with this awareness, Marcher continues to see his future as an extraordinary one: his fate is to be bankrupt, dishonoured, pilloried, events without any relation to what Marcher is in the present and with an accidental quality that absolves him of any responsibility for bringing them to pass.

Marcher does not appear to use his imagination to enrich the present by exploring the future; he does not know how to investigate the potentialities or select from the possibilities that the future offers to the present. He imagines the future in a way that isolates it from the present—the only quality which Marcher allows it is a strangeness sufficient to drain the present of any value which it may contain. Marcher's own image of the future is of an agency fully shaped in a way that he cannot specify, impinging at some point on his present and radically altering its shape. While the upheaval is to occur in time, its singularity, and its value for Marcher would seem to be in its indiscernibility; it cannot be prepared for and its eruption in time will be so sudden and of so short a duration that it will scarcely be known other than by its effects—the radical transformation it will leave in its wake.

> "It's to be something you're merely to suffer?"
>
> "Well, say to wait for—to have to meet, to face, to see suddenly break out in my life; possibly destroying all further consciousness, possibly annihilating me; possibly, on the other hand, only altering everything, striking at the root of all my world and leaving me to the consequences, however they shape themselves." (360)

Marcher uses his imagination as a weapon to ward off time, to keep the dangerous beast at bay. He does this by using his imagination to endow the future with independent agency and significance. Perhaps inadvertently, Marcher sets up a signpost prohibiting all exploration of that domain by consigning it to the unimaginable. When he does choose to use his imagination in time, it is, significantly, only to register his dissatisfaction with a meager past, apparently oblivious of any suspicion that the past is as much constituted by choices made in the present as a record of possibilities missed and experiences denied.

A past as insubstantial as Marcher's may be said to invite imaginative reconstruction and Marcher can, with safety, invest it with deeds of considerable dimension. In this vein, he wonders why he could not have saved May from a capsized boat, or at least recovered her dressing bag, filched by a lazzarone with a stiletto. The heroic self-portrayal is congenial to Marcher because the hero may be viewed as not responsible to the workings of everyday time. The hero, conceived as eternally young, can afford to scorn ordinary intimacies and everyday trivialities. If the hero is impervious to everyday time, it may be because his acts are performed to redress an upset, never of his own making, in ordinary time. To rescue someone from the unexpected is to prevent a dislocation of ordinary time and permit it to resume. When it does resume the hero withdraws (or the tale ends), hence his actions remain eternally fresh and vivid. The hero, in this interpretation, requires no past or future and need not be measured by ordinary time in which actions do have causes in the past and consequences in the future. His actions are fully completed when ordinary time resumes and luminously justified by its humdrum resumption.

In a cruel image, James proceeds to deny to the aging Marcher that any such heroic exemption from time exists.

> He had settled to his safety . . . figuring to himself, with some colour, in the likeness of certain little old men he remembered to have seen, of whom, all meagre and wizened as they might look, it was related that they had in their time fought twenty duels or been loved by ten princesses. (397)

In an important passage, James describes Marcher's present as a "simplification of everything but the state of suspense. That remained only by seeming to hang in the void surrounding it." (372) But even a state of suspense must draw from the future, or from the past, to maintain its vitality. And to the extent that Marcher may, at one time, have feared his future fate, or at the very least feared the possibility that others might find his fate ridiculous, the state of suspense could still be distinguished from the void—if James means by the void the devaluation of the past and future which surround Marcher's present.

It may indeed be because of his early fears that May agrees to watch with him, a willingness that Marcher undervalues because, unlike May, it is his future fate and not his present fears which fix and hold his attention. Unlike her companion, May is aware of the passage of time and her subjection to it. Marcher initially perceives her at Weatherend as having visibly aged. "She *was* there on harder terms than anyone; she was there as a consequence of things suffered, one way and another, in the interval of years. . . ." (353) Because she is conscious of the passage of time, May is primarily alert to Marcher's condition in the present. When she does consent to share Marcher's watch, it is only after having asked him three times whether he is afraid. The questions indicate that perhaps what most interests May is not the future in which Marcher alone is to meet his unique fate, but the present in which Marcher has needs that May can meet, needs that make him dependent on her for sympathy, understanding, and support. Marcher is baffled by May's questions because he conceives his relationship to May in the present as subordinate to and at the service of his singular destiny. By contrast May, grasping at straws, hazards that Marcher's destiny, with its by-product of fear that can be met and assuaged, may be used to develop and serve their relationship in the present.

When the question is later resumed between them, and Marcher's "original fear, if fear it had been, had lost itself in the desert" (372), May's watch is at an end and the present is indeed barren. There has been no growth in Marcher's awareness of his dependency upon May, and May's need for Marcher remains mute and unexpressed, for want of an answering voice. Without understanding why, Marcher senses that from that point on their discourse bears the mark of something finished and completed.

At Weatherend May's function was to explain to the curious the history of the place and the objects it shelters. These treasures, so full of history and poetry, have been tested by time, and their value once established, they are to be preserved against time. What is striking is Marcher's way of viewing his own destiny as though it were an object of similar worth. The stupid world is to be kept in deliberate ignorance of his singularity, and it is May, with her superior knowledge, who will be allowed "to dispose the concealing veil in the right folds." (367) She is to be both witness and keeper—and the value of that over which she watches is no more open to discussion than the more publicly recognized treasures at Weatherend.[4]

If Marcher refrains, with a fine show of detachment, from the display of greed which causes his associates to all but handle the objects presented to their view at Weatherend, he is much less circumspect in fingering that other treasure, his consciousness of his own unique fate. His carefully cherished image of his future fate resembles in many ways a work of art: it is the result of an imaginative effort, set apart from ordinary incomplete events, and endowed with its own intrinsic significance. But, unlike Marcher's fate, a work of art is specific. By choosing from a range of possibilities, excluding some in the process of giving meaning to others, a work of art is given its concrete charac-

[4] When Marcher finally understands that the beast has sprung, he learns it, James says, from *outside* his life, not from within. His life, like an object of art, has become endowed with a consistency and finality of its own. The knowledge jostled him "with the disrespect of chance, the insolence of accident." (401) Marcher, having carefully preserved himself against time, can no longer win to his truth through any effort or experience of his own. The knowledge he seeks is, ironically, given to him accidentally—with just the quality of irrelevancy, of might have been otherwise, that characterizes his own past.

teristics and this is what Marcher, in analogous circumstances, is unable or unwilling to do.

Likewise Marcher thinks himself disinterested, "even a little sublimely—unselfish" in carefully allowing for May's requirements and peculiarities. (364) But his studied consideration, James indicates, is really a mask for the purest egotism, the price Marcher consents to pay for the luxury of May's attention. Between the greed of the visitors at Weatherend and Marcher's more disingenuous selfishness there would appear to be far less difference than Marcher himself is able to perceive.

Whether he wishes it or not, Marcher lives in ordinary time. James describes Marcher's entanglement with ordinary time as involuntary and to a large extent unconscious, "a passage of his consciousness in the suddenest way, from one extreme to another." (364) Marcher's fate is not to understand, until too late, what such sudden passages signify: that Marcher *is* subject to ordinary time, and that what he figures to himself as perfect detachment will be seen, in the end even by Marcher, as perfect selfishness. When the Beast has sprung and Marcher is forced to see the real measure of his past "in the chill of his egotism and the light of her use" it is too late. (402) Unknown to himself he had lived, been measured, and found wanting—by ordinary time.

A Perspective on "The Beast in the Jungle"

by James Kraft

The exact nature of the relationship that John Marcher and May Bartram actually establish in Henry James's "The Beast in the Jungle" often escapes scrutiny amid contemplation of the lost possibilities in that relationship. John's and May's personalities shape and produce a unique attachment; certain basic needs bring them to each other, and the satisfaction of these needs perpetuates their relationship. If James makes or implies a judgment on John Marcher, and on May Bartram, it is one that is controlled by what does exist in the genuinely realized experience of their life together. . . .

It might help in explaining this perspective on the tale to consider here the scene from *The Ambassadors* in which Strether speaks to Bilham in Gloriani's garden. The novel was written before the tale, but the conception for the tale is recorded in James's notebook during the same year, 1901, in which he was writing the novel.[1] Of the two statements that are particularly relevant in this context, the first would seem to suggest a condemnation of the futility in the life of John Marcher and May Bartram.

> Live all you can; it's a mistake not to. It doesn't so much matter what you do in particular, so long as you have your life. If you haven't had that what *have* you had?

The second, less well known, is a part of the same speech of Strether. It indicates that the possibilities of one's life are seriously conditioned by the nature of one's consciousness, and implies that the judgment on the quality of an individual life cannot be made in absolute terms.

> The affair—I mean the affair of life—couldn't, no doubt, have been dif-

"A Perspective on 'The Beast in the Jungle,'" by James Kraft. From Literatur in Wissenschaft und Unterricht, *II (1969), 29–36. Reprinted by permission of the publisher.*

[1] *The Notebooks of Henry James,* ed. F. O. Matthiessen and Kenneth B. Murdock (New York, 1947), pp. 311–12.

ferent for me; for it's at the best a tin mould, either fluted and embossed, with ornamental excrescences, or else smooth and dreadfully plain, into which, a helpless jelly, one's consciousness is poured—so that one "takes" the form, as the great cook says, and is more or less compactly held by it: one lives in fine as one can.[2]

It is necessary to see the life of John Marcher and May Bartram in relation to this concept. John's neurotic, narrow preoccupation with the portentous event clearly results in an unrealistic and damaging existence. May is devoted to him and loves him, but her attitude also seems unrealistic and deficient when she continues to think that she can change him. Yet they do have a life together. They fill the vessel of their consciousness as only they can. We do not fail to see what limits them, but we must not fail to see that in life it does not so much matter what you do as long as you have had what life of yours there is to have. Our judgment on John and May must be as fine as the complexity that James's consciousness reveals to us. It is in the fineness of that consciousness that the morality exists.

Although the critics have indicated that the moral implications of the tale are clear, there is another possibility. We must be capable of seeing that within the definite limitations of their consciousness, John and May do create all the life that is possible for them. James does in one way condemn the two through his examination of their failure, but he also leads us to a point of observation from which we see that their life is not without value for them. John's final insight and May's love and function in helping him gain this insight, even after her death, may have been more productive for them—more truly creative—than we are willing at first to consider. One can only explore this possibility and realize that in making a decision about it one employs a personal judgment and, hence, perceives according to one's own needs. Here such a moral viewpoint is delicately balanced by the awareness of all the implications of life that continually fascinated the mind of James.

In order to clarify this point, the reader might consider L. C. Knights' essay, "Henry James and the Trapped Spectator."[3] Mr. Knights' purpose in this essay is twofold and he explains it in this way:

From an early period James was interested in persons whose free and normal development—the development that, given their endowment, one might have expected—is thwarted by the egotism of others. As he grew older that preoccupation was joined . . . by another—a preoccupation with the plight of the creature trapped not by others—but shall we say?

[2] Henry James, *The Ambassadors* (New York, 1909), I, 217, 218.
[3] In *Explorations* (London, 1946), pp. 155–69.

—by Fate; and some of his most notable stories present the trapped, the caged, the excluded consciousness.[4]

The aspect of Mr. Knights' discussion that is relevant here is the second, "the plight of the creature trapped" by his own limitations, a plight demanding our seeing the limitations of the creature, but also the actual condition of what he is. Mr. Knights briefly considers "The Beast in the Jungle" and the conclusion he draws from it, although not exactly like the one presented here, does suggest a similar attitude. His point is best made in discussing James's style: "One would like to attempt a definition of 'intelligence' and to relate it to James's style which, at its best, is a medium for projecting the immediate awareness if not of 'opposite and discordant' qualities at all events of varied and (in most minds) contradictory impulses, so that the reader's consciousness is enlarged to admit a new relationship."[5] He speaks of the "double burden" of this style that makes us see in our widened consciousness the complex structure of life. It is a sense of this double burden, of the contradictory impulses in life, that I suggest is necessary for a full understanding of "The Beast in the Jungle."

There is a passage from James's notebooks that could suggest this complex attitude James hopes to convey at the end of "The Beast in the Jungle." He is describing his visit in 1904 to the cemetery of his family in Cambridge, Massachusetts. The setting, his observation on his sister, whom he loved and cared for so much during her last illness, and his anguished realizations at her grave contain certain similarities to Marcher's condition and combine all the pity, the wonder, and the fear that seem to be the conflicting but deeply conceived emotions about life that James would have us bring together at the end of "The Beast in the Jungle."

Everything was there, everything *came;* the recognition, stillness, the strangeness, the pity and the sanctity and the terror, the breath-catching passion and the divine relief of tears. William's inspired transcript, on the exquisite little Florentine urn of Alice's ashes, William's divine gift to us, and to *her,* of the Dantean lines—

Dopo lungo exilio e martiro
Viene a questa pace—

took me so at the throat by its penetrating *rightness,* that it was as if one sank down on one's knees in a kind of anguish of gratitude before something for which one had waited with a long, deep *ache.* But why do I write of the all unutterable and the all abysmal? Why does my pen not

[4] Ibid., p. 162.
[5] Ibid., p. 168.

drop from my hand on approaching the infinite pity and tragedy of all the past? It does, poor helpless pen, with what it meets of the ineffable, what it meets of the cold Medusa-face of life, of all the life *lived,* on every side. *Basta, basta!* [6]

[6] *Notebooks,* p. 321.

The Ghost in the Jolly Corner

by Maxwell Geismar

"The Jolly Corner" . . . was a . . . highly personal and autobiographical document. In effect this was another of the Jamesian ghost tales in which one side of Henry James pursued—or was pursued by—another side of Henry James. Could anything be more complete—as a Jamesian id fancy—cozier, or more revealing? And in fact "The Jolly Corner" was a fascinating study of the Imperial Henry James tracking down his own ghost, his alter ego, or himself, in the upper floors of the deserted house which had once contained the "happy memories" of his childhood.

That was the central situation of the ghostly tale, which reverted in part to the psychological terror of *The Turn of the Screw,* and of a late tale which has been the subject of much critical speculation and interpretation. The hero is a man of fifty-six who, like the elderly exile of *The Ambassadors,* is too old to "live" any more, and has come back to New York, in this line of later Jamesian heroes, to rehearse his childhood experiences in a series of gossipy talks with a sympathetic confidante. (In this sense, now that the sexual barrier in James's work has been completely leveled by "old age," now when "good talk" is permissible as the *only* sexual link, these elderly, effeminate, gossipy Jamesian protagonists have just begun to live.) Spencer Brydon confides all this to Alice Staverton: that is, his speculations as to the financial titan he might have been if he had remained in America; and while, like the heroine of "The Beast in the Jungle," she reassures him about any possible "selfishness," or even morbidity on his part, he pursues his new obsession. For he still thinks that all things come back "to the question of what he personally might have been, how he might have led his life and 'turned out,' if he had not so, at the outset, given it up—

> Not to have followed my perverse young course—and almost in the teeth of my father's curse, as I may say; not to have kept it up so, "over there,"

"The Ghost in the Jolly Corner." From Maxwell Geismar, Henry James and the Jacobites *(Boston: Houghton Mifflin Company, 1963), pp. 355–64. Copyright © 1962, 1963 by Maxwell Geismar. Reprinted by permission of the author and the publisher.*

> from that day to this, without a doubt or a pang; not above all, to have liked it, to have loved it, so much, loved it, no doubt, with such an abysmal conceit of my own preference: some variation from that, I say, must have produced some different effect for my life and for my "form."

There is no doubt as to the personal, autobiographical reference to James's own career in this statement; the lingering consciousness of his own early conflict, choice, and exile. But this spokesman of "The Jolly Corner" is again careful to discriminate the purpose of his late obsession. "If I had waited . . . then I might have been, by staying here, something nearer to one of those types who have been hammered so hard and made so keen by their conditions." This was his reference, one assumes, to the new financial titans and monopolists; but—

> It isn't that I admire them so much—the question of any charm in them, or of any charm beyond that of the rank money-passion, exerted by their conditions *for* them, has nothing to do with the matter: it's only a question of what fantastic, yet perfectly possible, development of my own nature I mayn't have missed. It comes over me that I had then a strange alter ego deep down somewhere within me, as the full-blown flower is in the small tight bud, and that I just took the course, I just transferred him to the climate, that blighted him for once and for ever.

Thus, it was not a question of James (or his present hero) *preferring* America and New York life to the European existence which he had loved so much, without a doubt or pang. It was not a question, really, of choosing to have been one of the new robber barons whom he described so naïvely and in terms of floral growths. It was simply that he now felt capable of leading *both* lives; and this greedy ego could not forego any development of his own nature. In the story the sympathetic Miss Staverton agrees that this other flowering of the Jamesian temperament was possible, too. "I feel it would have been quite splendid, quite huge and monstrous." "Monstrous above all!" the hero echoes complacently, "and I imagine, by the same stroke, quite hideous and offensive." Would you like me to have been a billionaire? he asks her; to get her comforting reassurance, "How should I not have liked you?" And Spencer Brydon sets out to track down this Jamesian alter ego.

But note how often James himself now used the word "monstrous" himself, and how this insatiable fantasist is increasingly identified with the beastlike animals who figure in his own imagery of respectable, confined leisure-class life. Yet the ghostly atmosphere of "The Jolly Corner" is very well done; and high up in the house of childhood, in a series of connected rooms with the final room having no other outlet, the Jamesian ghost, tracked down, at bay, and bristling, makes its stand. "Brydon at this instant tasted probably of a sensation more complex than had ever before found itself consistent with sanity." He feels both pride and terror; pride that this other mask of himself is worthy of *him;* and terror indeed while, "softly panting, he felt his eyes almost leave their sockets." Those eyes—which have figured so largely throughout the voyeuristic pattern of James's work; and those high connecting "upper rooms" of the James family's house, which could very logically be the bedrooms about which a whole series of Jamesian "observers" have made their nocturnal tours.

Now what was *in* the locked room of the Jamesian unconscious? The conventional sociological interpretation, first expounded by Matthiessen, is simply that James was writing a parable of what might have happened to his own character if he had stayed in the United States. For, desperately fleeing back down the long stairway, this once omnipotent ghost-tracker is not spared a final glimpse of a monstrous, alien countenance, not his own; but a hideous ghost whose ethereal hand is marked by mutilated fingers. The alter ego of the Jamesian billionaire has been corrupted and disfigured; he is a stranger.

The conventional Freudian interpretation of the story, however, as perhaps best expounded by Clifton Fadiman, explicitly following, as this critic acknowledged, "Dr. Saul Rosenzweig's remarkable monograph, 'The Ghost of Henry James: A Study in Thematic Apperception,' " is on a much more personal level. It is based on Henry's mysterious wound or "obscure hurt" at the time of the Civil War, which prevented him "from joining in the masculine activity of making war," in Mr. Fadiman's words, and which also (probably) prevented him "from experiencing normal sex relations." Thus the early injury of James's is represented in the symbolically castrated fingers of the ghostly alter ego, and it symbolized a certain death in James, according to Mr. Fadiman, "the death of passion," while "The withdrawal to Europe, the most important outward event of his long life was another symbol of the retreat from the American experience that, in a sense, had been too much for him."

And, continuing with this theory of thematic apperception, these early wounds and repressions of Henry James's rose up to consciousness in later life (this is perhaps a Jungian touch) and his last visit to the United States was a compulsive act to relive this ancient trauma. (The orthodox Freudian repetition-compulsion.) "As Dr. Rosenzweig so persuasively puts it," added Mr. Fadiman glowingly, the visit " 'was largely actuated by an impulse to repair, if possible, the injury and to complete the unfinished experience of his youth.' " James wrote the story all unconsciously, we are told finally, and quite correctly; but it is obvious "that James's ghosts anticipate and dramatize many of the findings of psychoanalysis."

Here again, James is being hailed as the (unconscious) father of the

Freudian thought which all of our findings tend utterly to disprove. He was indeed the sublime example of classical face-saving rationalization which completely avoided the least vestige of the Freudian truths. During the course of these speculations (in Mr. Fadiman's *Short Stories of Henry James*), we are also told that "The Jolly Corner" is one of the most difficult of James's last stories:

> Composed in his famous final manner, it serves as a fair example of the complexity of his mind, a complexity that forced him (as with Joyce and other innovators) virtually to invent a style.

Well, we have noticed that later Jamesian style whose "complexity" was often invented to cover a virtual absence of content. And this large statement represents an entire range of false, fatuous and grandiose claims which are recurrently made about James's work. His mind, as should be clear at this point of our study, was not so much "complex" as very often incredibly naïve. Once you have established the Jamesian hierarchy of values (strange as they are in any realistic appraisal of life), this famous mind becomes indeed almost conventional or trite—certainly clever or ingenious rather than profound. In one sense we can state categorically that Henry James *never had an idea.*

Mr. Fadiman has again joined the bewitched, bemused and Circe-ish circle of Jacobite commentators, at the loss, momentarily, one hopes, of his own normal intelligence. For there was no "death of passion" in James's life or career, simply because he had never reached the point of passion. His whole view of sex and love was on the oral, infantile, pre-oedipal and pre-sexual level. His own attitude is consistently that of the pubescent (at best) voyeur, "spying out" the hidden, mysterious, and ultimately sinful, area of "adult intimacy."

There was no "second death" in Henry James's withdrawal to Europe, simply because it was America which was always "death" to James. It was Europe which was, from his earliest literary fantasies of fame and the "good life," right down to the repeated affirmation of this theme by the divided hero in "The Jolly Corner" itself—it was Europe which was life, life, life to James. He could not possibly have returned to America to work out, to resolve these earlier traumas, because it is obvious throughout his career and his work that these traumas were buried deeply under layer upon layer of sublime rationalization. In his own life he possibly never even understood that there was a trauma—and in his work, as we have now seen, every issue of depth psychology was always resolved by a sentimental, romantic kind of "psycho-morality"—that is, when James was consciously aware of these issues at all. No, James returned to America simply to *confirm,* to expand, to applaud and to celebrate the whole purpose of his own

European pilgrimage—as *The American Scene* shows without question; as the end of "The Jolly Corner" also proclaims. The only trouble with the Rosenzweig-Fadiman thesis is that, while fitting James into the conventional Freudian categories, it shows no knowledge of James's real motivation or temperament.

What was behind the locked door in the empty room of the Jamesian temperament—the room to which the omnipotent searcher of "The Jolly Corner" had pursued his psychological prey—was *the Jamesian unconscious.* (One should remember the early, recurrent dream of the young James during which he is chased down the long, empty corridors of an art museum by the hideous specter of his anxiety—only to turn upon, and to *defeat* this ogre by the sheer force of his will to power and to fame.) What lurked at bay in this empty, locked room was simply perhaps the real author of *The Sacred Fount*; or the artist who set down the curious oedipal-incestuous central situation in *The Golden Bowl*—and then refused to see it; or the writer-creator of a whole long series of neurotic, morbid, even hysterical "narrator-observers" in the Jamesian fiction who still persisted in denying the true nature of his own primary literary spokesmen. "Do you believe then—too dreadfully!—that I *am* as good as I might ever have been?" asks Spencer Brydon of "The Jolly Corner" in all the false modesty which covers his persistent, dominant concern with himself alone. But this monster egotist is still too clever, too self-protective, ever to stir—to *really* question—those hidden psychological depths lying deep down—not far up—within him.

The manner of this hero's "escape" from the repressed part of his own temperament is also interesting. For he surrenders abjectly. He is devoured by the necessity to "see" this hidden "monster"—to discover that in which "all the hunger of his prime need might have been met, his high curiosity crowned, his unrest assuaged." But he grasps at the idea of a saving, an inexorable and vital "discretion":

> Discretion—he jumped at that; and yet not, verily at such a pitch, because it saved his nerves or his skin, but because, much more valuably, it saved the situation. When I say he "jumped" at it I feel the consonance of this term with the fact that—at the end indeed of I know not how long—he did move again, he crossed straight to the door. He wouldn't touch it—it seemed now that he might *if* he would: he would only just wait there a little, to show, to prove, that he wouldn't. He had thus another station, close to the thin partition by which revelation was denied to him; but with his eyes bent and his hands held off in a mere intensity of stillness. He listened as if there had been something to hear, but this attitude while it lasted, was his own communication. "If you won't then—good: I spare you and I give up. You affect me as by the appeal positively to pity: you convince me that for reasons rigid and sublime—what

do I know?—we both of us should have suffered. I respect them then, and, though moved and privileged as, I believe, it has never been given to man, I retire, I renounce—never, on my honour, to try again. So rest for ever—and let *me!*"

But wasn't this saving "discretion" the complete key to the Jamesian fiction throughout his long career: the discretion of a gentleman, say, though not of a major artist? What a fascinating passage this was indeed: since it was also the perfect self-projection of the Jamesian temperament and achievement alike. Wasn't the "saving of the situation" a key theme in James's work—the saving of "face," too, as in *The Golden Bowl,* by pretending in all one's respectable middle-class American virtue that the situation, which was there, did not exist? (Not to mention the *other,* deeper situation, also so consistently there in the novel, and just as consistently denied by James, and described as filial or parental love.) Hovering by the closed door of the Jamesian unconscious, this hero—like so many other Jamesian figures back to the sensitive young Anglo-American observer in *The Portrait of a Lady*—"wouldn't touch it," though he might if he would! This hero, in the typically Jamesian vein, simply "waits," he listens, he "watches," though now with his eyes bent, and his hands held off, for the "revelation" which is there, and which is denied to him. He retires; he "renounces"—in the best Jamesian resolution of all the great problems and issues of life; I mean of living. And still he reasserts his own authority, his own ego, his own terrified but deeply covered, protected, and impenetrable self-image, by feeling that "appeal positively to pity." He is both moved and privileged, by what he has *not* seen, as no man before him. "I spare you and I give up." What a happy, face-saving and ego-saving solution; which still leaves the weight of the decision not upon the menacing Jamesian unconscious, but upon *him!* What then of "those reasons"—rigid indeed, if not possibly or entirely "sublime"—by which both halves of the divided Jamesian temperament might have suffered if they had become clear? "So rest for ever—and let *me!*"

Again the final accent was on the Jamesian "I," the "Omnipotent Me," who has come to the edge of his own darkness, and then has retreated frantically, even hysterically—but still with "dignity," and with immutable "self-possession." The hero of "The Jolly Corner" does think fleetingly of suicide, by escaping from his demon through the upper-floor window *without* a ladder. He yearns for "some comforting common fact, some vulgar human note, the passage of a scavenger or a thief, some night-bird however base." And why are these symbolic associations of dirt, crime and baseness linked so directly here with the "vulgar human note"? Did the Jamesian snobbery penetrate so deeply even into these unconscious areas of his temperament? Or was this the *true* imagery of his buried self? Retreating down the long stairway of his childhood, of his family's empty and haunted house, this hero also is forced to catch at least a fleeting glimpse (which is exactly what one does catch in James's best work) of "the monster with the mutilated fingers"—or of, shall we say, the inhibited Jamesian "id." He faints and falls upon the floor. "They were cold, these marble squares of his youth"—and where indeed is the "Jolly Corner" of James's younger American experience?

Yet even this brilliant self-portrait, perhaps the best and most accurate description of James's whole body of literary work—as compared with the apologetic, the evasive, the self-glorifying "Prefaces"—was muffled again by the "false" (that is to say, the *conscious*) ending of the story. The hidden self of the Jamesian hero is indeed "monstrous." It is "evil, odious, blatant, vulgar"—James's worst terms of abuse. But it is surely, this hero thinks, the "face of a stranger"—as indeed it was in James's work. And though the gentle, good, tactful Alice Staverton accepts the possible explanation that it *might have been* this hero's personality, if he had remained in America; and she accepts the maimed specter also because it is his, Spencer Brydon's—she comforts him with "the cool charity and virtue of her lips." That "charity and virtue," in truth, which is also a synonym, in James's work, for "discretion" or "pity" or "waiting" or "watching" or "retiring" or "renouncing"—for all these barely concealed modes of nonrecognition, evasion, and flight as the "resolution" for the fleeting depth insights which appear indeed so hideous and so horrid to this neurotic and repressed late-Victorian artist who then rationalized and even glorified the obvious process of his literary sublimation.

Universality in "The Jolly Corner"

by William A. Freedman

H. G. Wells once likened the reading of a piece of James's fiction to entering a great cathedral, walking awesomely down the aisle, and finding at last on the altar, a dead kitten, egg shell, a bit of string. The implication is obvious: For Wells, as for many others, James was much ado about nothing; he had no message, not even any worthwhile ideas to offer. However, as more recent scholarship than will bear citation has shown, James's fiction is certainly not devoid of ideas. And, I suggest, while it may not be socially ameliorative, neither is it always without a message. Any message in James's fiction is of course not likely to be presented as such; it is not didacticized, for James deplored the use of art for purposes of overt moral instruction. Instead the message will be carefully woven into the texture of the work, and the weave must often be deliberately undone before it can be found. It is my intention in the next few pages to play Penelope with "The Jolly Corner."

"Everyone asks me what I *think* of everything," said Spencer Brydon, "and I make answer as I can—begging or dodging the question, putting them off with any nonsense." This is the opening sentence of "The Jolly Corner," and as is almost always the case with James's first sentences, it carries a special weight. For the recurrence of universal quantifiers, here "Everyone," "everything," and "any," presages the prevasive appearance of a vocabulary abounding in such exhaustives. The word *all,* for example, appears no fewer than sixty-six times, ten times in the combination *above all.* And when we add to this the number of appearances of *ever* and *every* (sixteen), *everything* (ten), *any* (thirteen), *anything* (five), *whole* (eight), *never* and *none* (fifteen), and *nothing* (ten), we are provided with a vocabulary of generalizations which makes up a large part of the fictional and ideational pattern of the story. James's fiction, existential at least to this extent, rests on the premise that existence precedes essence. For James, terms often had no

---

pre-existent essence or meaning, and the work of art itself was necessary to establish it. As a result, meanings are supplied by and emerge from the stories themselves. On one level, this explains the abundant use of this all-encompassing, hence indefinite, terminology. From the first, Spencer Brydon knows that for him "everything" is some sort of self-knowledge. Thus, with regard to everyone's asking him what he thinks about everything, he remarks: "It wouldn't matter to any of them really, . . . for, even were it possible to meet in that stand-and-deliver way so silly a demand on so big a subject, my 'thoughts' would still be almost altogether about something that concerns only myself." "He found all things come back to the question of what he personally might have been." Yet it is not until much later that he is to discover, to define as it were, the "might have been," and it is thus labeled only as "all things" or "everything." At the moment of perception, therefore, when the object of his quest has been literally and figuratively cornered, "everything" and "everyone" become "something" and "somebody": "It gloomed, it loomed, it was something, it was somebody, the prodigy of a personal presence." The all-inclusive has become particular, hence meaningful. To affix a label of "something" or "somebody," however, is still not to define fully, and while this figure of the Spencer Brydon that might have been is subsequently described in some detail, he turns out not after all to have been the search's ultimate end: Recovering in the lap of Alice Staverton from his swoon of self-perception, Brydon "had come back, yes—come back from further away than any man but himself had ever travelled; but it was strange how with this sense what he had come back *to* seemed really the great thing, and as if his prodigious journey had been all for the sake of it." And what he has come back to is Alice Staverton, the woman he had left thirty years before, along with a chance for a prodigious fortune, to pursue a prodigal existence on the continent. Thus the final specific definition for Spencer Brydon of "all," of the "everything" and "everyone" of the first sentence is having Alice and being himself—as he is. And it is contained in the final lines of the story, thereby completing the unravelment of the cognitive tapestry: " 'He [the Brydon that might have been] has a million a year,' he lucidly added. 'But he hasn't you!' 'And he isn't—no, he isn't—you!' she murmured as he drew her to his breast." In this sense, therefore, "The Jolly Corner" represents an untypically jolly counterpart to James's "The Beast in the Jungle." John Marcher, the passive protagonist of that story, has missed his "everything." By waiting inactively for his something big to happen, his beast to spring, Marcher has missed the one positive thing in his life—the love he might have shared with May Bartram. As a result, the positive something for which he had waited all his life and which had become for him an obsessive "everything" emerges as "Nothing" itself: ". . . he had been the man of his time, the man to whom nothing on earth was to have happened. That was the rare stroke—that was his visitation." Spencer Brydon, on the other hand, has confronted his beast in the jungle. He has stalked and trapped the monster (the imagery is even more consistent with the jungle motif) he might have been, and having done so, he has won the prize which evaded John Marcher. He has won Alice Staverton, the May Bartram of "The Jolly Corner"—his everything.

The sweeping language of "The Jolly Corner" does more than point up and define the significance of self-knowledge to Spencer Brydon. The constant references to "all," "everyone," "everything," and the like, make the reader feel that more than Spencer Brydon and his unique situation is involved here. It gives him a sense of universality about the story. At first blush, it may appear that Brydon's tale is a bit too unique for broader application. After all, not many of us have had the opportunity to turn down a million dollars or more in favor of even an urbane prodigality. But Brydon himself dispels the surface particularity:

> If I had waited I might have seen it was, and then I might have been, by staying here, something nearer to one of these types who have been hammered so hard and made so keen by their conditions. It isn't that I admire them so much—the question of any charm in them, or of any charm, beyond that of the rank money-passion, exerted by their conditions *for* them, has nothing to do with the matter: it's only a question of what fantastic, yet perfectly possible, development of my own nature I mayn't have missed.

The question, then, is reduced to a consideration of what aspect of himself, what alter ego, has never reached fruition. Surely this is a question we all may, and perhaps do, with curiosity share.

There are indications other than the language of totality that James intended us to share it. There is, in addition, terminology distinctly reminiscent of and metaphorical allusions to three of the greatest sources of symbolic and allegorical reference in all literature: *The New Testament,* Dante's *Divina Commedia,* and Plato's *Republic,* Book VII—"The Allegory of the Cave." Thus Brydon's "coming to" following his great perception and resultant swoon is variously described in terms of Lazarus' revivification by Jesus (" 'Yes—I can only have died. You brought me literally to life. Only,' he wondered, his eyes rising to her, 'only, in the name of all the benedictions, how?' "); Dante's return from the Inferno ("He had come back, yes—come back from farther away than any man but himself had ever travelled; but it was strange how with this sense what he had come back *to* seemed really the great thing, and as if his prodigious journey had been all for the sake of it"); and the Philosopher-King's vision of the Good ("It had brought him to knowledge, to knowledge—yes, this was the beauty of his state."). There are other references to *The New Testament.* For example, the scene delineated at this coming to—Spencer Brydon lying effete, his head cushioned in the lap of Alice Staverton, Mrs. Muldoon "kneeling on the ground before him"—irresistibly evokes the picture of Christ's descent from the cross. The word, "descent," in fact, describes his return, "charity," "virtue," and "beatitude" his recognition of her love—" 'And now I keep you,' she said." As for *Divina Commedia,* there is, in addition to the above, the reference to the incipient appearance of the monstrous spectre as "The penumbra, dense and dark, . . . the virtual screen of a figure which stood in it as still as some image erect in a niche or as some black-vizored sentinel guarding a treasure." But it is Plato's famed "Allegory of the Cave" with which "The Jolly Corner" exhibits the most consistent affinities. In fact, the house on the jolly corner is, *mutatis mutandis,* an analogue of the cave, just as the overwhelming perception of the monstrous self that might have been is, with the necessary qualifications, an analogue of the vision of the Good. To trace the many relationships would require a full-length study and I will not attempt to do it here. A few of them, however, are worth noting. The open rooms of the house appear to Brydon as "mouths of caverns," and there is but a single light-admitting aperture; Brydon carries a candle which casts shadows, creating the illusion of "an apparitional world"; and the objects of his search, "the old baffled foresworn possibilities," are referred to as "Forms." As regards the perception, it takes place in one of the "upper rooms"; it is a "vision," "mystic," of an "ineffable identity," and it brings him "to knowledge," knowledge Platonically defined as "beauty."

Now, I am not at all suggesting that James's "The Jolly Corner" is an allegory of Plato's allegory (art thrice removed, as it were). These are analogues and similarities, not one-to-one correlations, and there are also, of course, distinctions. The vision is, after all, of an aspect of Brydon's self, not of eternal Form or Truth; it is, though it brings him to knowledge, monstrous rather than magnificent (though Plato warns that there will be a shock of recognition); and the perception is not, like the perception of the Good, an end in itself, but a means—though a very necessary means—to a greater end (the discovery of Alice Staverton). Nevertheless, it is, I hope, clear, that when Brydon complains that "Everyone asks me what I *think* of everything," and when James tells us that Brydon found "all things come back to the question of what he personally might have been," there is, in these universals, no mere evasiveness. There is a strong suggestion that somewhere or other everyone's got a jolly little corner of his own, and that he might do well to investigate it someday.

Chronology of Important Dates

	Henry James	*Historical and Cultural Events*
1843	Henry James born April 15, Washington Place, New York City.	
1850		Hawthorne's *The Scarlet Letter.*
1855	Family moves to Europe.	
1861	Family returns to Newport, R.I. James is injured and cannot enlist.	Civil War breaks out.
1862	Enters Harvard Law School.	Emancipation Proclamation. Turgenev's *Fathers and Sons.*
1864	First story published.	
1865		Civil War ends.
1870		Franco-Prussian War.
1871		George Eliot's *Middlemarch.*
1874	Spends a year in Europe and returns to New York.	First Impressionist Exhibition, Paris.
1875	Lives in Paris; meets Flaubert, Zola, Turgenev.	
1876	Settles in London. *Roderick Hudson* appears in book form.	
1878	*Daisy Miller.*	
1881	*The Portrait of a Lady.*	

1890–95	Writes unsuccessfully for the London stage. Publishes "The Pupil" (1891), "The Real Thing" (1892).	William James's *The Principles of Psychology* (1890).
1896	"The Figure in the Carpet."	
1898	*The Turn of the Screw.*	
1900		Freud's *The Interpretation of Dreams.*
1902	*The Wings of the Dove.*	The Triple Alliance. William James's *The Varieties of Religious Experience.*
1903	*The Ambassadors,* "The Beast in the Jungle."	Entente Cordiale. Wright Brothers' aeroplane flight.
1904	Revisits the U.S. *The Golden Bowl.*	Henry Adams' *Mont St. Michel and Chartres.*
1907	*The American Scene.*	*The Education of Henry Adams,* William James's *Pragmatism.*
1908	"The Jolly Corner."	
1914	*Notes of a Son and Brother.*	World War I breaks out.
1915	James becomes a British citizen.	Einstein's General Theory of Relativity.
1916	Receives the Order of Merit. Dies in London, February 28.	Easter Rebellion in Dublin. James Joyce's *A Portrait of the Artist as a Young Man.*

Notes on the Editor and Contributors

JANE P. TOMPKINS is a student of Melville's prose style and has written an article on James's late style. She teaches English at Temple University.

CHARLES FEIDELSON, JR., Professor of English and director of American Studies at Yale University, is the author of *Symbolism and American Literature.* He has edited the Rinehart Edition of *Moby Dick,* and co-edited collections of essays on American literature and the backgrounds of modern literature.

WILLIAM A. FREEDMAN has written articles on Shakespeare, Fielding, Whitman, Dreiser, Faulkner, Steinbeck, Trilling, and Malamud. He is a Senior Lecturer at Haifa University in Israel.

MAXWELL GEISMAR, critic and historian of American letters, is the author of *Henry James and the Jacobites.* He has completed the first three volumes of a projected five-volume history of the American novel, and has edited anthologies of the works of several American authors.

HAROLD C. GODDARD was Professor of English and former head of the English department at Swarthmore College. His works, published posthumously, include *The Meaning of Shakespeare, Atomic Peace,* and *Blake's Fourfold Vision.*

ELISABETH HANSOT, Assistant Professor of Political Science at Columbia University, is preparing for publication a study on utopian thought.

JAMES KRAFT, Assistant Professor of English at Wesleyan University, is the author of *The Early Tales of Henry James,* and of several articles on American literature.

EARLE G. LABOR has written articles on Stephen Crane, Henry Green, Ernest Hemingway, and Jack London. He is Professor of English at Centenary College, Shreveport, Louisiana.

SEYMOUR LAINOFF, born in Hamburg, Germany, teaches English at Yeshiva University. He has written on Wordsworth, Kafka, and Turgenev, and is the author of a critique of "The Real Thing" not included in this volume.

TERENCE MARTIN, Associate Professor of English at Indiana University, is the author of *The Instructed Vision: Scottish Common Sense Philosophy and the Origins of American Fiction.*

M. SLAUGHTER teaches English linguistics at the University of California at Santa Barbara. Her dissertation, which is being revised for publication, is entitled "The Universal Language Movement in the Seventeenth Century."

WILLIAM BYSSHE STEIN, a professor at the State University of New York at Binghamton, has written articles on Thoreau and Stephen Crane, and is the author of *Hawthorne's Faust: A Study of the Devil Archetype*.

DAVID TOOR, who teaches English at the State University of New York at Cortland, is a novelist and short story writer whose most recent critical work has dealt with Robert Frost and James Joyce.

Selected Bibliography

Beebe, Maurice, and Stafford, William T. "Criticism of Henry James: A Selected Checklist." *Modern Fiction Studies,* XII (Spring, 1966), 117–77.

Dupee, F. W. *Henry James.* New York: Delta Publishing Co., Inc., 1951. The best short biographical and critical study of James.

Edel, Leon. "The Tales." In *Henry James: A Collection of Critical Essays,* edited by Leon Edel, pp. 172–79. Twentieth Century Views. Englewood Cliffs, N.J.: Prentice-Hall, Inc., 1963. Sketches James's development as a writer of short fiction.

Kimbrough, Robert, ed. *The Turn of the Screw.* New York: W. W. Norton & Company, Inc., 1966. Contains an authoritative text of the tale, useful background and source materials, and a variety of critical essays.

Stone, Edward. *Seven Stories and Studies.* New York: Appleton-Century-Crofts, Inc., 1961. Contains four of the stories discussed in this volume and excerpts from some articles not reprinted here.

Vaid, Krishna. *Technique in the Tales of Henry James.* Cambridge, Massachusetts: Harvard University Press, 1964. Provides a useful summary of the narrative methods in James's short fiction, and offers detailed discussions of several tales, including "The Pupil," "The Figure in the Carpet," "The Beast in the Jungle," and "The Jolly Corner."

Willen, Gerald, ed. *A Casebook on Henry James's The Turn of the Screw.* New York: Thomas Y. Crowell Company, 1960. Provides a wide-ranging assortment of critical essays on the tale, a selective bibliography, and exercises for students.

TWENTIETH CENTURY INTERPRETATIONS

MAYNARD MACK, *Series Editor*
Yale University

NOW AVAILABLE
Collections of Critical Essays
ON

ADVENTURES OF HUCKLEBERRY FINN
ALL FOR LOVE
THE AMBASSADORS
ARROWSMITH
AS YOU LIKE IT
BLEAK HOUSE
THE BOOK OF JOB
THE CASTLE
CORIOLANUS
DOCTOR FAUSTUS
DON JUAN
DUBLINERS
THE DUCHESS OF MALFI
ENDGAME
EURIPIDES' ALCESTIS
THE FALL OF THE HOUSE OF USHER
A FAREWELL TO ARMS
THE FROGS
GRAY'S ELEGY
THE GREAT GATSBY
GULLIVER'S TRAVELS
HAMLET
HARD TIMES
HENRY IV, PART ONE
HENRY IV, PART TWO
HENRY V
THE ICEMAN COMETH
JULIUS CAESAR

(continued on next page)

(*continued from previous page*)

Keats's Odes
Light in August
Lord Jim
Major Barbara
Measure for Measure
Merchant of Venice
Moll Flanders
Much Ado About Nothing
The Nigger of the "Narcissus"
Oedipus Rex
The Old Man and the Sea
Pamela
A Passage to India
The Playboy of the Western World
The Portrait of a Lady
A Portrait of the Artist as a Young Man
The Praise of Folly
Pride and Prejudice
The Rape of the Lock
The Rime of the Ancient Mariner
Robinson Crusoe
Romeo and Juliet
Samson Agonistes
The Scarlet Letter
Sir Gawain and the Green Knight
Songs of Innocence and of Experience
Sons and Lovers
The Sound and the Fury
The Tempest
Tess of the D'Urbervilles
Tom Jones
To the Lighthouse
The Turn of the Screw and Other Tales
Twelfth Night
Utopia
Vanity Fair
Walden
The Waste Land
Women in Love
Wuthering Heights

TWENTIETH CENTURY VIEWS

British Authors

JANE AUSTEN, edited by Ian Watt (S-TC-26)
THE BEOWULF POET, edited by Donald K. Fry (S-TC-82)
BLAKE, edited by Northrop Frye (S-TC-58)
BYRON, edited by Paul West (S-TC-31)
COLERIDGE, edited by Kathleen Coburn (S-TC-70)
CONRAD, edited by Marvin Mudrick (S-TC-53)
DICKENS, edited by Martin Price (S-TC-72)
JOHN DONNE, edited by Helen Gardner (S-TC-19)
DRYDEN, edited by Bernard N. Schilling (S-TC-32)
GEORGE ELIOT, edited by George R. Creeger (S-TC-90)
T. S. ELIOT, edited by Hugh Kenner (S-TC-2)
FIELDING, edited by Ronald Paulson (S-TC-9)
FORSTER, edited by Malcolm Bradbury (S-TC-59)
HARDY, edited by Albert Guérard (S-TC-25)
HOPKINS, edited by Geoffrey H. Hartman (S-TC-57)
A. E. HOUSMAN, edited by Christopher Ricks (S-TC-83)
SAMUEL JOHNSON, edited by Donald J. Greene (S-TC-48)
BEN JONSON, edited by Jonas A. Barish (S-TC-22)
KEATS, edited by Walter Jackson Bate (S-TC-43)
D. H. LAWRENCE, edited by Mark Spilka (S-TC-24)
MARLOWE, edited by Clifford Leech (S-TC-44)
ANDREW MARVELL, edited by George deF. Lord (S-TC-81)
MILTON, edited by Louis L. Martz (S-TC-60)
MODERN BRITISH DRAMATISTS, edited by John Russell Brown (S-TC-74)
RESTORATION DRAMATISTS, edited by Earl Miner (S-TC-64)
SAMUEL RICHARDSON, edited by John Carroll (S-TC-85)
SHAKESPEARE: THE COMEDIES, edited by Kenneth Muir (S-TC-47)
SHAKESPEARE: THE HISTORIES, edited by Eugene M. Waith (S-TC-45)
SHAKESPEARE: THE TRAGEDIES, edited by Alfred Harbage (S-TC-40)
G. B. SHAW, edited by R. J. Kaufmann (S-TC-50)
SHELLEY, edited by George M. Ridenour (S-TC-49)
SPENSER, edited by Harry Berger, Jr. (S-TC-80)
LAURENCE STERNE, edited by John Traugott (S-TC-77)
SWIFT, edited by Ernest Tuveson (S-TC-35)
THACKERAY, edited by Alexander Welsh (S-TC-75)
DYLAN THOMAS, edited by Charles B. Cox (S-TC-56)
OSCAR WILDE, edited by Richard Ellmann (S-TC-87)
YEATS, edited by John Unterecker (S-TC-23)